Sew Many Gifts, Sew Little Time

Sew Many Gifts, Sew Little Time

More Than 50 Special Projects To Be Cherished & Enjoyed

Chris Rankin

A Sterling/Lark Book
Sterling Publishing Co., Inc. New York

Photography: Evan Bracken, Light Reflections
Production: Elaine Thompson
Art Director: Kathleen Holmes
Editor: Dawn Cusick
Proofreading: Julie Brown
Illustrations: Charlie Covington

Library of Congress Cataloging-in-Publication Date
Rankin, Chris.
    Sew many gifts, sew little time : more than 50 special projects to be
cherished & enjoyed / Chris Rankin.
      p.   cm.
    "A Sterling/Lark book."
    Includes index.
    ISBN 0-8069-0606-5
    1. Sewing.   2. Gifts.   3. Needlework--Patterns.   I. Title.
TT715.R36   1994
746.4--dc20   93-44538
                                         CIP

10 9 8 7 6 5 4 3 2 1

A Sterling/Lark Book

Published in 1994 by Sterling Publishing Co., Inc.
387 Park Avenue South, New York, NY 10016

Produced by Altamont Press, Inc.
50 College Street, Asheville, NC 28801

All photos and projects not credited on page 126 © Ariadne/Spaarnestad,
Utrecht, Holland. Instructions translated by Networks, Inc. English
translation © 1994, Altamont Press.

© 1994, Altamont Press

Distributed in Canada by Sterling Publishing
   c/o Canadian Manda Group, P.O. Box 920, Station U
   Toronto, Ontario, Canada M8Z 5P9
Distributed in the United Kingdom by Cassell PLC
   Villiers House, 41/47 Strand, London WC2N 5JE, England
Distributed in Australia by Capricorn Link (Australia) Pty Ltd.,
   P.O. Box 6651, Baulkham Hills, Business Centre, NSW 2153,
   Australia

ISBN 0-8069-0606-5

CONTENTS

INTRODUCTION

Giving the perfect gift is one of the greatest pleasures in life; unfortunately, finding the perfect gift is one of life's greatest challenges. For sewers, though, who frequently have an abundance of fabric and creative energy, gift giving becomes simple when they're presented with a few project ideas.

The projects in this book represent a continuum of gifts for a variety of occasions and every type of person on your list. For those practical personalities, you can make a tool holder, a travel case, sewing and art bags, a beach blanket, and even a chess set. For those on your list who adore pretty trinkets and treasures, there's a sachet bag, a heart wreath, a wallhanging, notecards, and a whimsical wind kite. For the young people on your list, there are gifts like a fold-up pillow quilt and miniature teddys to play with, and gifts like an alphabet bed set, applique beach towels, and color-ful kitchen ware to make everyday living more fun.

Many of the projects are accompanied by full-size patterns. In cases where the patterns are too large to show full-size, you're given a reduced pattern and instruc-tions for increasing the pattern to its correct size. Years ago, enlarging patterns was usually done with grid paper and a lot of patience; today, just find an enlarg-ing photocopying machine (print shops are a good source if your library doesn't have one), and enlarge the pattern by the percentage indicated in the text.

Feel free to adapt the patterns and projects as your imagination sees fit. The wind kite on page 51 may work perfectly for a teenager if you substitute trans-ferred color photos of a favorite rock band for the dogwood motifs. The bathroom basket on page 54 might be adapted to make a magazine basket for Uncle Max by using different fabrics and a larger basket. The bicycle tool holder on page 38 could be rearranged to form an organizer for a baby stroller. However you choose to use this book, be sure to make a few won-derful gifts for yourself, too. You deserve them.

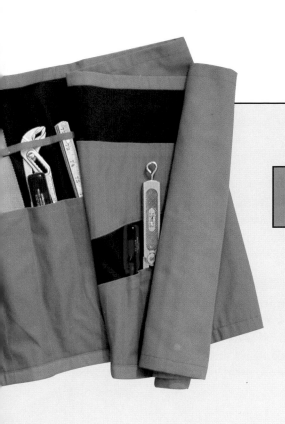

PRACTICAL PLEASURES

PRACTICALLY SPEAKING, EVERYONE LOVES A GIFT. UNFORTUNATELY, NOT EVERYONE WILL LOVE THE SAME GIFT. IF YOU FIND YOURSELF WORRYING ABOUT ACHIEVING THE CORRECT FIT, WHETHER THEY'LL FIND THAT DAINTY LACE EDGING ATTRACTIVE, OR IF THE GIFT WILL JUST SIT ON A SHELF SOMEWHERE COLLECTING DUST, THEN LOOK THROUGH THIS CHAPTER FOR GIFT IDEAS. ALTHOUGH MOST OF THE PROJECTS WERE DEVISED TO SERVE A SPECIFIC FUNCTION — ORGANIZING TOOLS, KNITTING NEEDLES, OR ART AND SEWING SUPPLIES — THE PROJECTS CAN BE ADAPTED TO SUIT THE SPECIAL INTERESTS AND HOBBIES OF YOUR GIFT RECIPIENT.

CRAZY QUILT PURSE

Here's your chance to enjoy the pleasures of crazy quilting without investing several months in a full-size bed quilt. Although many of the most memorable historical crazy quilts were made in velvets and brocades, cotton works just fine for small projects such as this one.

 Cotton print scraps in several colors, 12-inch (30 cm) square of white cotton, embroidery floss, zipper, 10-1/4 x 10-3/4 (26 x 27 cm) rectangle of lining fabric

Cut out the cotton scraps in any shapes you like, using the photo as a guide. Baste the shapes to the 12-inch square of fabric, overlapping the fabrics as you work. Stitch the pieces in place with two strands of embroidery floss in a buttonhole or overhand stitch. Remove the basting threads and use the lining fabric as a pattern to cut out the crazy quilt patchwork.

Fold the crazy quilt square right sides together and sew the side seams. Turn right sides out. Fold the lining in half with right sides together and sew the side seams. Make a hem along the upper edges and insert the purse with wrong sides together. Fold a 1/4-inch (6 mm) hem along both long sides and sew in the zipper, leaving 1/4 inch on each edge. Tack along the zipper edges.

CHESSBOARD,
DICE BAG,
AND COASTERS

These simple projects make the perfect gift for game players. For a special young person, consider making the chessboard as a checkers board and filling the dice bag with checkers. The projects can be finished in an afternoon, so you may want to make several at a time.

CHESSBOARD

3/4 yard (.7 m) each of blue, red, and yellow felt

Cut out 32 2-inch squares of yellow felt. Cut out the red felt to a 16-inch (40 cm) square, and the blue felt to an 18-3/4-inch (47 cm) square.

Place the red felt in the center of the blue felt and hand baste. Then pin the yellow squares in a chessboard pattern and zigzag them in place. Last, zigzag the outer edges of the red squares and remove the basting stitches.

A.J. Gillam

SCHAKE
VOOR BEGINNE

INLEIDING TOT
HET SCHAAKSPEL

onder redactie van Paul van der Sterren

DICE BAG

6- x 16-3/4-inch (15 x 42 cm) rectangle of blue cotton, scrap of white cotton with black dots (or scrap of white cotton and a black permanent marker), fusible interfacing, white shoelace

Cut out three squares of the white polka dot fabric. Round the corners and cut out interfacing to match. Fold the blue cotton in half lengthwise. (The fold will form the lower edge of the bag.) Iron the white cotton squares to the front of the bag.

Fold the blue cotton with right sides facing and sew the side seams. Press the top 1-1/2 inch (4 cm) down and top stitch in place. Make a casing at the top of the back by sewing lines 3/4 inch and 1 inch (2 and 2.5 cm) from the upper edge, leaving a small opening at one seam. Thread in the shoelace, gather, and tie.

COASTER

Scraps of felt in assorted colors, including white

Cut out the white felt in 4-inch (10 cm) squares and spread them out with their right sides facing up. Cut out the remaining colors of felt in squares, triangles, or border patterns, using the photo for inspiration. Position the shapes onto the white felt squares and zigzag them in place. To finish, zigzag around the outside edges of each coaster.

TRAVEL CASE

*With pockets for all the useful road gadgets —
a tire gauge, a compass, pen and mileage log
book, a magnifying glass, and a map — this
project makes the perfect gift for travellers.
If your gift recipient never logs gas mileage,
fill that space with a bag of peanuts or a
favorite candy.*

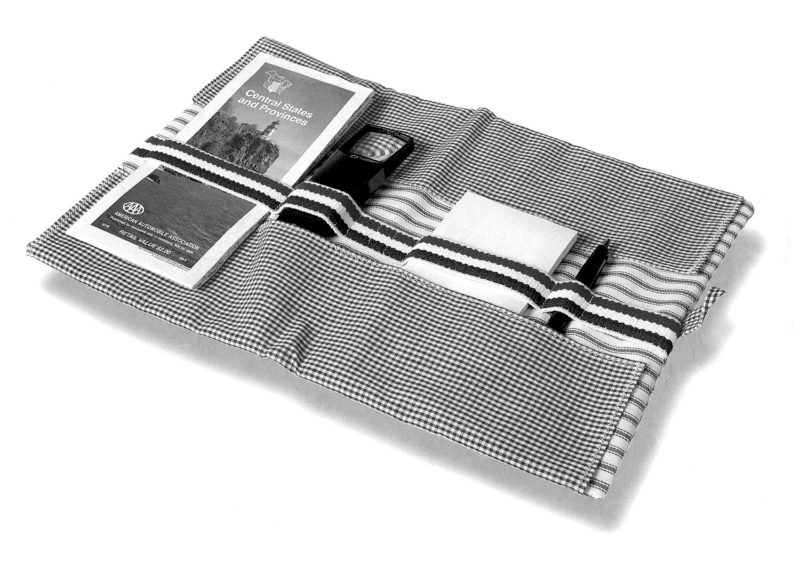

1/4 yard (.2 m) cotton fabric,
1/4 yard contrasting cotton fabric,
button, cardboard

Cut two rectangles measuring 16-1/2 x 11-1/4 (42 x 28 cm) for the outside of the case and two rectangles measuring 15-1/4 x 5 inches (39 x 12 cm) for the contrasting flaps. Plan the placement of the items you plan to insert in the case.

Gently stretch and topstitch the elastic across one of the large rectangles of fabric about 4-1/2 inches (11.5 cm) up from the bottom of one of the long edges.

Press and hem one of the long edges and both short edges of the smaller fabric rectangles. Fold a strip of fabric measuring 1/2-inch wide x 1-1/2 inches long (1.25 x 11.5 cm) in half with right sides together and stitch the long edge. Turn right sides out and press. Fold the tube in half to form a loop.

Pin the loop on the second large rectangle with the raw edges in the seam area and the loop facing away from the fabric. Pin the flap pieces (the smaller rectangles) in place with right sides facing, with one of the flap pieces covering the loop. Sew the two long and one short side seams. Turn right sides out and press.

Position the button so it will line up with the loop and sew in place. Cut out two pieces of cardboard measuring 10-1/4 x 7 inches (26 x 18 cm) and insert them into the larger rectangles, leaving the excess space in the center open so the case will fold in half. Slipstitch the opening closed.

flap

cardboard

cardboard

flap

21

INSULATED CASSEROLE CARRIER

Part of the fun of this casserole carrier is the designer's choice of a fresh, fun print, as opposed to the traditional check or striped print. The batting provides heat insulation, while the foam core protects wood surface from heat marks.

1 yard (.9 m) outer fabric (preferably cotton), 1 yard contrasting fabric for the lining, 1 yard 1/2-inch (12 mm) thick batting, 3 yards (2.7 m) double-fold bias tape (or bias strips cut from one of the fabrics and a bias tape-marker), 3 snaps, 2 wooden dowels 12 inches (30 cm) long and 3/8 inch (9 mm) in diameter, 3/8-inch thick rectangles of foam core measuring 8 x 11 inches (20 x 28 cm)

Cut out the fabrics according to the diagrams. (Be sure the fabrics have been prewashed to prevent any shrinkage in the finished project.) Baste the batting to the wrong side of the outer fabric to form the main carrier piece. Machine stitch the batting to the outer fabric just inside the seam line with a long zigzag stitch. Trim the batting close to the stitching.

Cut two pieces of bias tape to 20 inches (50 cm) for the ties. Turn in the ends of each piece and fold the pieces in half lengthwise. Stitch close to the double-folded edges. Center one tie end on the right side of the 10-inch side of the flap section, 3 inches (7.5 cm) in from one end. Stitch the end securely in place.

With right sides facing, pin each flap section to a flap lining section, leaving one of the short edges unpinned and keeping the ties free. Stitch, slightly rounding the corners. Trim the seams, turn right sides out, and press. Baste across the open edge. Hem one long edge of the pocket section with a 1/2-inch double hem. Fold the seam allowance to the wrong side on the other long edge and press.

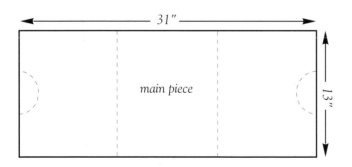

main piece — 31" — 13"

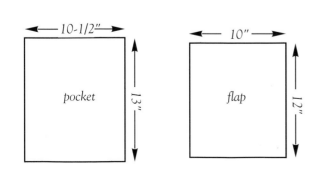

pocket — 10-1/2" — 13"

flap — 10" — 12"

Position the pocket right side up on the right side of the main piece, centering it between the ends with the short edges of the pocket aligned with the long edges of the main piece. Stitch the pocket to the carrier along the outer edges. On the long, unhemmed edge of the pocket, stitch to close the fold that you pressed earlier.

Cut out a 5-1/2-inch (14 cm) paper circle to use as a template for the openings at the carrier ends. Fold the circle in half and center it on one short end of the main piece, with the template's straight edge aligned with the fabric's edge. Trace the outline of the template onto the fabric, taking care to position the semicircles in the exact same place to ensure they will line up, then repeat the process on the other end of the carrier and with both ends of the lining piece.

Stitch along the marked lines, then cut out the semicircles 1/8-inch (3 mm) inside the stitched lines. Bind each curved edge with bias tape.

Place the outer section of the carrier right side up on a table. Center a flap section with its lining side facing up, on each long edge of the carrier, aligning the raw edges and keeping the ties free. Then place the carrier lining with its wrong side facing up, on top. Pin the layers together, then stitch around all sides, taking care to securely backstitch at the cutout edges. Trim the corners, turn right sides out through the cutout opening, and press. Sew a snap to the inner binding at the center of each cutout, and sew another snap at the center of the pocket's hem, close to the edge. Slip the dowels into place at the ends of the carrier, and slide the foam core in its pocket.

PAINT BAG

This practical gift bag makes a lovely present for artists of all ages and skill levels. For a more elaborate gift, fill the bag with an inspiring selection of paints and brushes.

16-inch (40 cm) square piece of cardboard, black fusible interfacing and black cotton fabric, each measuring 10 x 8-3/4 inches (25 x 22 cm), 3 lengths of ribbon in assorted widths, 8-inch (20 cm) black zipper

Cut the ribbons to 8-3/4- and 10-inch lengths. Pin the interfacing to the cardboard, then pin the shorter ribbons to the upper edges of the interfacing. Next, pin the longer ribbons to the sides of the interfacing and weave through the vertical ribbons until the interfacing is covered. Iron the ribbon to the interfacing. Fold the cotton and interfacing in half, right sides together, and sew the side seams. Turn right sides out, and sew the zipper to the upper edge.

LUNCH BAG

"Brown-bagging" takes on a new realm of colorful possibilities when your lunch bag is made from fabric. To make the bag larger or smaller, just find a paper bag with the right dimensions and use it as a pattern.

 1/2 yard (.45 m) main fabric, 1/2 yard lining fabric, 1/2 yard insulation fabric (terry cloth, batting, or an old towel), 2-inch (5 cm) hook and loop fastener, paper bag the size you'd like your finished lunch bag to be

Cut open the center crease of the paper bags's sides and across the center bottom. Cut along the remaining short crease to the corners and press the bag flat. (You should have a rectangle with the two bottom corners missing.)

Add seam allowances to the paper bag pattern and cut out two each of the fabric, lining, and insulation fabrics, marking the corners as they occur on the paper bag. Cut out a flap from the main fabric measuring 4 x 6 inches (10 x 13 cm).

With right sides facing, sew the side and bottom seams. Press the seams open. For each bottom corner, bring the edges of the corner opening together, matching the side and bottom seams, and stitch the seam straight across. Baste the insulation piece to the wrong side of the lining piece, and trim so the insulation fabric is slightly inside the seam line. Sew the lining fabric as you did the main fabric.

Pin the two bags together with right sides facing and stitch them together, leaving about 3 inches (7 cm) open for turning. Turn right sides out and press, then topstitch close to the edges. Center the flap along one seamless side with one edge about an inch (2.5 cm) from the lip of the bag and the remaining flap hanging out over the edge. Stitch securely in place. Fold the top of the bag down to the desired depth and mark matching spots for the hook and loop placement. Stitch the hook and loop in place.

BRAIDED BARRETTE

These simple hair decorations look especially nice when made from scraps of velvets, flannels, and brocades. For a thicker barrette, you can braid the gold cord on top of a third tube of fabric. For a child's barrette, ribbon streamers can be tacked on the back side.

 3-1/2-inch (8 cm) barrette base, 2 fabric scraps cut to 3 x 8 inches (7 x 20 cm), 8-inch (20 cm) length of gold ribbon or cord, old stockings with their toe and hip portions cut off or other stuffing material, safety pin

Fold each piece of fabric in half lengthwise with right sides together and stitch along the long end to form a tube. Attach a safety pin to one end of the stocking leg and use it to pull the stocking through the fabric tube. Do not stretch the stocking unless you want a bunched-up effect.

Trim the protruding length of stocking about 1/2 inch (13 mm) beyond each end of the tube. Push the excess stocking into the tube. Fold each end under about 1/2 inch and stitch closed.

Tack the tubes and the gold cord together at the top. Braid the fabric and gold braid together as far down as you can and then tack the ends together. Attach the braid to the barrette by turning the stitched ends under and tacking each end to the barrette. Adjust the braid and tack it down the length of the barrette.

LACE PIN CUSHIONS

Pin cushions trimmed with antique lace edging make a special gift for sewers who love lace. Antique trims can be acquired inexpensively by searching antique stores for lace-trimmed clothing that's in bad shape and removing the lace.

 Scraps of linen, antique lace edging (purchased lace may be substituted), stuffing

Cut out two pieces of linen for each pillow, in either 4-inch (10 cm) squares or in circles traced from a saucer plate. With right sides facing, baste the lace edging to one of the linen shapes. Pin the remaining piece of linen with right sides facing. Stitch all around the shape, leaving an opening just large enough for turning. Turn right sides out, stuff well, and slipstitch the opening closed.

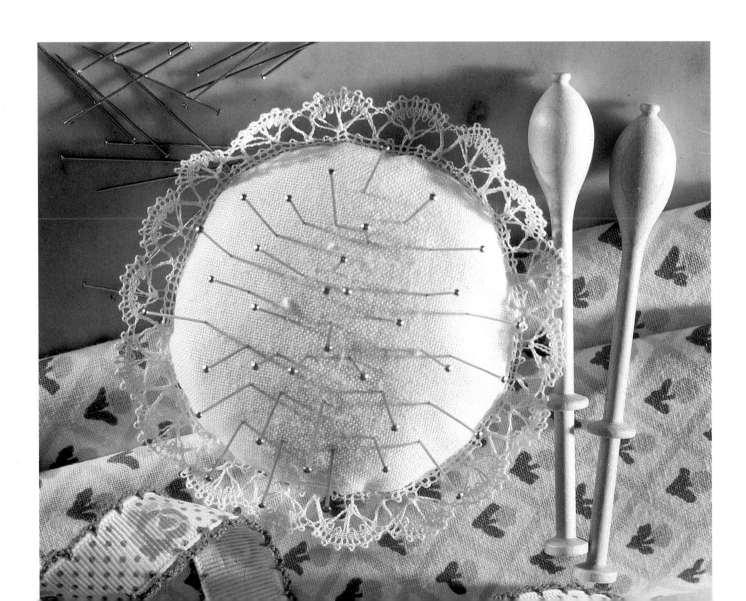

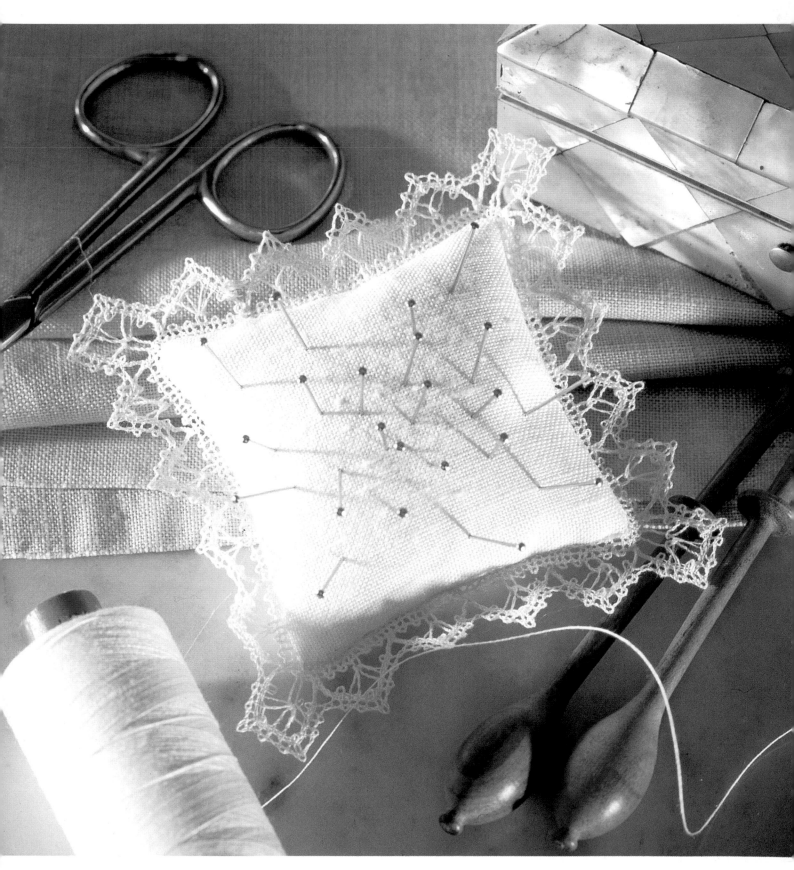

ROLL-UP KNITTING CASE

This gift is a wonderful way to help your favorite knitter keep track of her needles. The same instructions can also be used to make roll-up holders for other purposes, such as a utensil holder for picnics, an art supply organizer for budding artists, etc.

 1/2 yard (.45 m) print cotton fabric, 1/2 yard solid cotton fabric, 1/2 yard fusible interfacing, purchased binding or bias strips cut from the solid color fabric

Cut out one rectangle measuring 15 x 19 inches (38 x 48 cm) from both fabrics and the interfacing. Round the top two corners of the narrow edge of all three pieces, using the curve of a dinner plate as a guide if needed. Iron the interfacing to the print fabric.

With wrong sides facing together, bind the two fabrics on the short, uncurved edge. With the print fabric facing down, fold the bound edge up about 7 inches (18 cm) and press in place. Bind the remaining three edges. Measure off dividing spaces 1 to 1-1/2 inches wide (2.5 to 4 cm) with a chalk pencil or disappearing ink pen and stitch. Make a 24-inch (61 cm) tie from the binding or bias strips and tack it to the center of the print fabric.

BEACH SPREAD

Create this colorful beach spread from inexpensive scraps of terry cloth. The spread is pieced like a log cabin quilt, and the finished spread is lightweight enough to travel well and provide years of leisure time pleasure.

 Batting and lining fabric, both 58 inches (1.45 m) square, 1-1/4 yards (1.1 m) each of 13 colors of terry cloth

Cut out the terry cloth to the following dimensions: 1 color measuring 8-3/4 inches (22 cm) square; 4 colors measuring 8-3/4 x 16-3/4 inches (22 x 42 cm); 4 colors measuring 8-3/4 x 32-3/4 inches (22 x 82 cm); and 4 colors measuring 8-3/4 x 48-3/4 (22 x 122 cm).

Following the chart, sew the squares and rectangles together with 1/4-inch (6 mm) seam allowances. Press all seams open. Place the top and back fabric right sides together with the batting pinned to the wrong side of the top. Sew around all edges, leaving an opening large enough for turning. Turn the spread right sides out and hand-stitch the opening closed. Machine quilt the spread if desired.

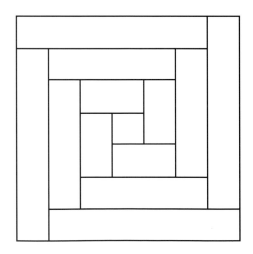

PLACE SETTING

This unusual place setting lets you arrange the utensils and place mats hours long before guests arrive. After the utensils are removed, the utensil holder folds out to an ordinary lap napkin.

1-1/2 yards (1.4 m) print fabric, 1 yard (.9 m) quilt batting

Create patterns by tracing the outline of your dinner plate onto a piece of paper and adding 1/4 inch (6 mm). Trace the plate again, this time adding 1-1/2 inches (4 cm) all the way around. For each place setting, cut out one smaller circle of fabric, two smaller circles of batting, and two larger circles of fabric.

Sew the two larger circles together with right sides facing, leaving a small opening for turning. Turn right sides out, handstitch the opening closed, and press. Clip and press the edges of the smaller circle under 1/4 inch. Trim the batting to match and baste it to the smaller circle. Blindstith or topstitch the smaller circle to the center of the larger one.

For the napkin and utensil holder, hem all four sides of a 21- x 20-inch (53 x 50 cm) rectangle of fabric and make a buttonhole as indicated on the pattern. Fold it as you would a napkin. Mark the area through one layer of fabric with pins where you'd like the utensils to rest. Cut out one of the napkin pieces from the pattern and hem all four sides. Open up the napkin and topstitch the utensil piece in place. Divide the space into three equal section and top-stitch.

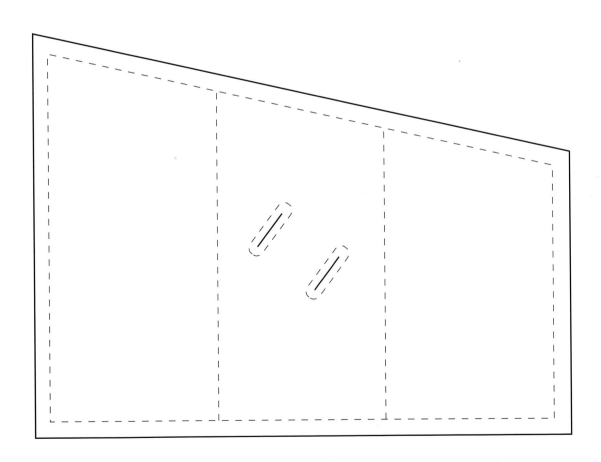

BIKE ORGANIZERS

*The pleasure and fun of bicycle travel
increases when your bike is stocked with
maps, tools, and snacks. Although the ones
shown are for adults, most children would
also like organizers for their bikes.*

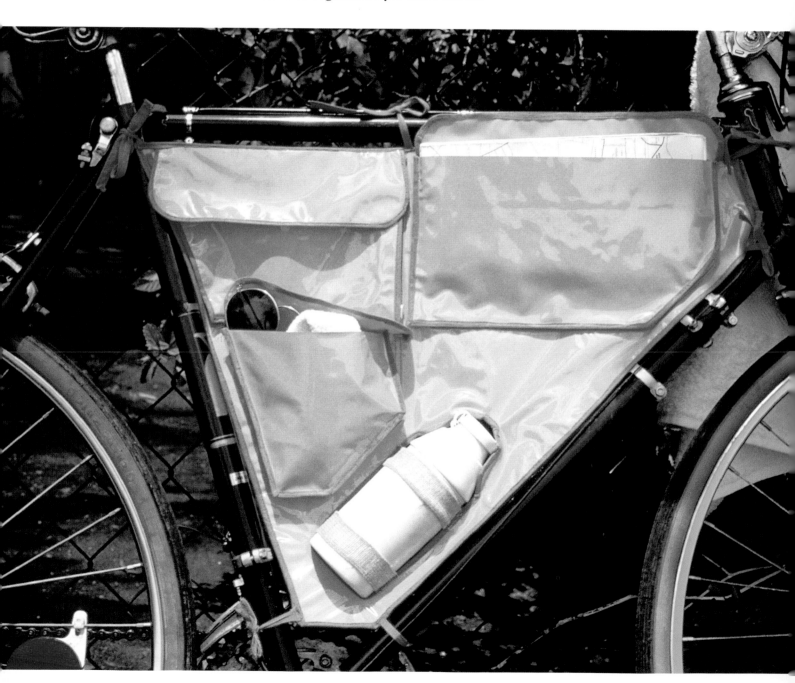

Old newspaper, 1-1/2 yards (1.4 m) waterproof fabric, Velcro closures, 8 yards (7.2 m) double-fold seam binding, 2 stretchy head bands for optional water bottle holder

First create a pattern to custom-fit your bicycle by tracing the space between the bars onto a sheet of newspaper. Cut out the pattern and fold it under 1/2 inch (12 mm) on all edges and then on the bottom corner so the organizer will clear the sprocket.

Gather the materials you'd like to make pockets for, such as maps, water bottle, tools, snacks, change purse, etc. Group together any of the smaller items that could be stored in the same pocket. Trace the individual shapes of all the items onto paper and add 1/2 inch for seam allowance. Cut out these shapes — which will become the pocket patterns — and fold the seam allowances under.

Place the patterns for the items on top of the main bike pattern and play with the arrangement of the patterns until you're pleased with the look. Trace the placement of the pocket patterns onto the main pattern.

Unfold the seam allowances from the pocket patterns and cut them out from the fabric. If flap are desired, cut a 3-inch (7 cm) flap with a 1/2-inch seam allowance and an extra 1/4 inch (3 mm) on both sides for rain protection. Cut out the main pattern shape, unfolding the seam allowance before you cut. For the pocket sides, measure the total length of the bottoms and sides of all the pockets, add about 10 inches (25 cm) for error, and cut out a strip of fabric that is the total length and 2 inches (5 cm) wide.

Cut lengths of the pocket strips to match the sides and bottom of each pocket. Join each pocket to the side and bottom with wrong sides together in a 1/2-inch seam. Trim to 1/4 inch and bind the edge with binding. Next, bind the top edge of each pocket front and strip. Turn the remaining edge of the strip under 1/2 inch. Round the two corners of the flap that will hang over, then bind all edges of the flap. Stitch the pressed edge of the pocket sides to the base according to your design. The flap should be stitched just above the top of the pocket.

Note: Extra attention is needed to form the water bottle pocket. First, add an extra 1/4 inch to the pattern and trim the edges with binding. To secure the bottle in place, fit the two head bands around the bottle, adjusting the fit with a seam. Stitch the opposite sides of the headbands to one side of the binding; use double stitching to add strength. Space the bands to allow for easy removal of the bottle and within 2 inches of the bottom to prevent the bottle from sliding out.

To attach the organizer to the bike, hold the organizer against your bike and measure from the edge around the bike's frame to the panel. If you plan to tie the organizer onto your bike, cut 12 2-inch-wide strips as long as the measurement from above plus 6 inches (15 cm).Fold the ties in half, turn the edges in to meet the center of the fold, and stitch the folded edges together. Stitch the two ties securely to the panel. If you plan to attach the panel with Velcro, cut 6 2-inch-wide strips as long as the measurement from above plus 1 inch. Bind the edges and stitch one edge of each strip to the panel. Then attach the Velcro.

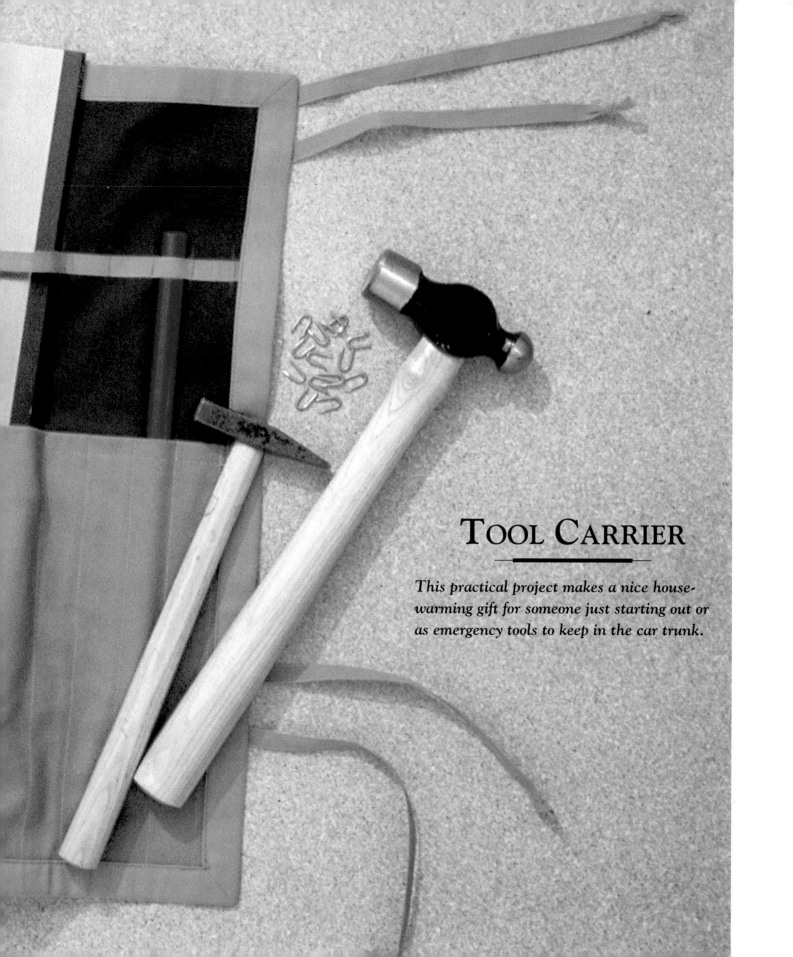

TOOL CARRIER

This practical project makes a nice house-warming gift for someone just starting out or as emergency tools to keep in the car trunk.

1/2 yard (.5 m) light blue fabric, 3/4 yard
(.7 m) dark blue fabric, 1/2 yard green
fabric, 3 yards (2.7 m) 1/4-inch (6 mm)
light blue seam binding, chalk pencil

Using the graph as a guide, cut out the pockets from
the green cotton with a 3/4-inch (18 mm) seam
allowance. Draw vertical lines for the pockets onto
the fabric with a chalk pencil. Make hems on the top
edges of both pockets, and position the large pocket
on the dark blue fabric so that the lower and side
edges are even. Sew through all the vertical lines.
Sew on the small pocket as indicated.

Sew the seam binding across the top edge of the
small pocket, then sew the vertical lines. Center the
dark blue fabric with wrong sides facing the light blue
fabric. Fold the edges to the inside with a small inner
hem, mitering the corners. Sew the hem. Fold the
rest of the narrow band in half, and sew the pieces on
one side seam, using the photo as a guide.

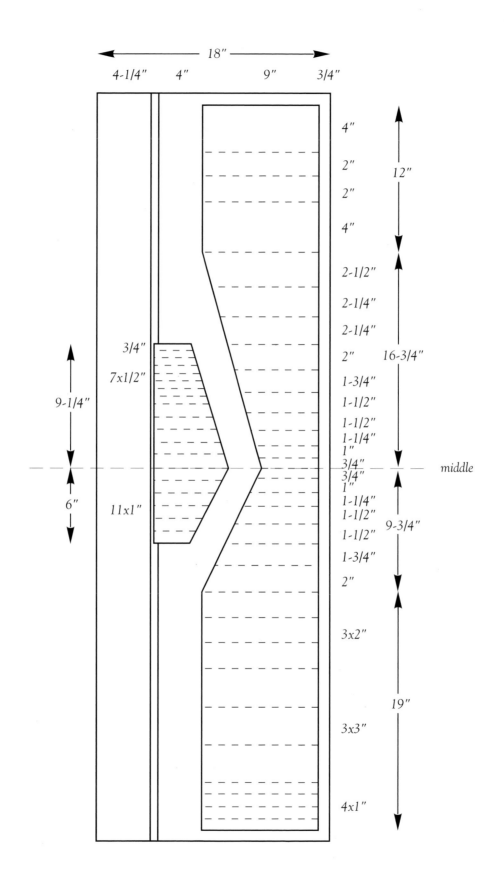

FANCIFUL FAVORS

PEOPLE DON'T MIND ACKNOWLEDG-
ING THAT GIVING A GIFT IS PURE
PLEASURE IN ITSELF, BUT SEWERS
RECEIVE EXTRA PLEASURE IN CRE-
ATING A GIFT. MANY OF THE PRO-
JECTS IN THIS CHAPTER — THE
QUILTING PROJECTS, FOR EXAMPLE
— GIVE YOU A GRAND EXCUSE TO
PLAY WITH SUCH FUN MATERIALS
AND TECHNIQUES AS LACE, RIBBON,
QUILT PIECING, AND RUFFLE GATH-
ERING. MANY OF THE PROJECTS ARE
SIMPLE ENOUGH TO MAKE WHILE
YOU ENJOY A FAVORITE TELEVISION
SHOW, REQUIRING MINIMAL TIME
AND TECHNICAL ATTENTION,
WHILE OTHERS WILL PROVIDE YOU
WITH A SATISFYING SENSE OF
ACCOMPLISHMENT AS YOUR WORK
TRANSFORMS FROM A PILE OF FAB-
RIC SCRAPS INTO A WONDROUS
COMPLETED PROJECT.

APPLE APRON

The waistline and length of this colorful apron can be custom fit to anyone, and the pattern can also be used to make matching potholders, place mats, or curtains.

1 yard (.9 m) of fabric for skirt, 2/3 yard (.6 m) of apple red fabric, scraps of green and brown print fabric, 12-inch (30 cm) square of quilt batting, 2 12-inch squares of white cotton fabric, monofilament and cotton thread

From the 1-yard fabric piece, cut a rectangle measuring 29 x 44 inches (74 x 112 cm); cut two strips measuring 5 x 44 inches (12 x 112 cm) from the red fabric, two strips measuring 2-1/2 x 44 inches (6 x 112 cm) from the red fabric, one strip measuring 2-1/2 x 12 inches (6 x 30 cm), and two waistband strips measuring 2-1/2 inches wide x the waistline measurement from the red fabric. Cut the apple, leaf, and stem motifs from the red, green, and brown fabrics.

Enlarge the apple motifs 114% and appliqué them to one of the white cotton squares. Form a quilt sandwich with the unappliquéd square of fabric on the bottom with its right side facing down, the batting in the middle, and the appliquéd square with its right side facing up on the top. Pin the binding through all three layers on the top edge of the square and sew it in place. Press a 1/4-inch (6 mm) seam allowance on both sides of the 2-1/2 x 44-inch strips. Fold the strip in half, wrong sides together, and press again. Position the end of each strip against the bottom side edge of the square and sew. The top portion of the strips will become the ties for the neck.

To attach the waistband to the bib, center the two waistband strips on the bottom edge of the bib, with the strips extending beyond the bib on either side. Match the edges, making sure the right sides are together. Sew across the entire length. Turn the strips down and press. Gather the top of the skirt until it fits the waistband and sew it to the front section of the waistband. Turn to the back and turn under a 1/4-inch seam on the back side of the band. Hand stitch in place.

Hem each of the 5- x 44-inch strips along their long sides and across one end to form the apron's waist ties. Pleat the raw end of the ties and sew into each end of the waistband. Hem each long side of the large fabric rectangle, and then turn up a 4-inch (10 cm) hem on one of the shorter sides.

POTHOLDER

 2 12-inch squares of white cotton fabric, scraps of red, brown, and green fabric, 12-inch square of quilt batting

Follow the instructions for making the top of the apron, binding on all four edges. Attach a loop for hanging.

WIND KITE

With this whimsical gift, you may choose to skip the wrapping paper and secretly hang it on the front porch or on a tree branch outside the gift recipient's window. As with many of the other motif projects in this book, feel free to adapt a shape from a magazine or book if the dogwood pattern won't work for you.

1/2 yard (.4 m) off-white fabric, 1/4 yard (.2 m) quilt batting, small scraps of applique fabrics, several colors of moire ribbon, 5-inch (12 cm) diameter wire ring, narrow satin ribbon

Cut out two rectangles measuring 11-1/4 x 12-1/2 inches (28.5 x 32 cm) from the fabric and one from the batting. Cut out the dogwood motifs. Position the motifs on the right side of one of the fabric rectangles and applique with a zigzag stitch around the edges. Baste the three rectangles together with batting in the middle and the fabrics' right sides facing out. Machine quilt in the pattern of your choice.

Sew the side seams with a 1/4-inch (6 mm) seam allowance with right sides together and press well. Press the top and bottom edges down 1/4 inch. Press the top edge down 1/2 inch (12 mm), slide the ring under the fold, and topstitch. Cut two lengths of narrow ribbon to 12 inches (30 cm) and stitch them across from each other on the top edge for hangers.

Cut the ribbon streamers to the desired length (4 to 5 feet, 1.2 to 1.5 m, is a popular length). For an extra touch, you may like to zigzag the outer edges of the ribbon in a matching or contrasting color. Press the bottom edge under 1/2 inch, pin the streamers in place, and topstitch.

BATHROOM BASKET

This basket makes a wonderful housewarming gift. It can be filled with any number of companion gifts — bath oils, homemade soaps, potpourri — to create a very personalized gift.

 7- x 12-inch (18 x 30 cm) market basket, 1/2 yard (.4 m) quilted fabric in a neutral color, 1/2 yard cotton print, 42 inches (1 m) of 3-tier lace in a color that complements the print fabric, 12 inches flat lace, 24 inches (60 cm) narrow ribbon, glue gun

Cut out the quilted fabric as indicated on the diagram at left. Sew the four corner seams together with right sides together. Turn right sides out and slip the cover up over the outside of the basket. Secure the fabric around the top of the basket with hot glue.

Cut out a 16- x 21-inch (40 x 53 cm) rectangle from the print fabric and round the corners. Gather outside edge to fit around the top of the basket. Let the print rest over the outside of the basket and glue it in place on top of the quilted fabric.

Glue the three-tier lace around the top of the print fabric. Place the 12-inch piece of flat lace in the center of the handle and glue. Tie bows on each side of the handle.

QUILTED NOTE CARDS

These quilted note cards make a more personal statement than any store-bought card. Using special fabrics, such as scraps from a wedding or christening gown, adds an extra touch. If you're feeling ambitious, give several cards in combination with the quilted purse on page 12.

 Several colors of printed cotton scraps, 5-1/2-inch (14 cm) square of white cotton, embroidery floss, heavy paper or cardboard, craft knife, white tape, writing paper

Cut out the cotton in assorted shapes and sizes. Baste the shapes to the white cotton square, overlapping the edges. Sew them in place with two strands of embroidery floss in a decorative buttonhole or overhand stitch, using the photo as a guide. Remove the basting thread.

Fold the cardboard or heavy paper in half. Cut out a 2-1/4- x 4-1/4-inch (5.5 x 11 cm) rectangle on the front of the card. Tape the quilted fabric inside the cutouts and tape over the back of the quilted fabric. Position the writing paper and glue it in place.

LACE VEST

Vests are becoming an increasingly popular part of our wardrobes, probably because they're so easy to dress up or down, depending on your mood or need. This vest requires minimal time and expense.

Vest pattern with lining, fabric yardage called for in pattern, contrasting fabric called for in pattern for lining, 2 yards (1.8 m) of two different lace trims, lace doilies in assorted shapes (or shapes cut out from applique lace yardage), monofilament and matching threads

Cut out the vest and then position the lace and the doilies to the front and back pieces. Hand baste the lace in place, taking care to match the lace trims on the side and the front pieces. Stitch by machine with monofilament thread. Finish assembling the vest as directed in the pattern instructions. Press well.

FRAGRANT SACHET

Sachet bags are a great project to use up scraps of leftover fabrics. You can fill the sachet with a store-bought potpourri or mix up a recipe from one of the recipes below that are based on historic plant meanings.

 16-inch (40 cm) square of cardboard, white fusible interfacing and white cotton fabric, both measuring 12 x 8 inches (30 x 20 cm), 4 lengths of ribbon in assorted widths

Cut the ribbons into 8- and 12-inch lengths. Pin the interfacing to the cardboard. Pin the shorter ribbons to the upper and lower edges of the interfacing, and then pin the longer ribbons to the sides of the interfacing. Weave through the vertical ribbons until the interfacing is covered, and iron the ribbon to the interfacing. Place the cotton and interfacing right sides together and sew the side and bottom seams together. Turn right sides out. Machine stitch the top edge down 1/4 inch (6 mm). Press the top down 1 inch (2.5 cm) to form a casing for the top. Top stitch the casing 3/4 inch (18 mm) from the top, leaving a small opening to thread in the drawstring ribbon.

A Symbolic Potpourri to Celebrate a Graduation

Cherry Blooms (good education)

Holly (foresight)

Scotch Fir (elevation)

Saffron (beware of success)

Sweet Basil (good wishes)

A Symbolic Potpourri to Celebrate a New Baby

Pussy Willows (unrealized promise)

Bachelor's-Buttons (single blessedness)

Parsley (festivity)

Moss (maternal love)

Honeysuckle (sweetness of disposition and bonds of love)

A Symbolic Potpourri to Celebrate a New Home

Eucalyptus (protection)

Sage (domestic virtue)

Cedar (strength)

Chamomile (energy in adversity)

Locust (elegance)

QUILTED COMFORTS

The simple, historical Dresden plate pattern is a pleasure to piece. The center circle is appliqued in place, so there're no difficult curved seams.

PILLOW

1 yard (.9 m) main fabric (for ruffle and back), scraps of four prints contrasting with the main fabric, 2 15-1/2-inch (40 cm) squares of off-white fabric, 15-1/2-inch square quilt batting, 14-inch pillow form, monofilament and matching threads

Cut four petals from each of the four print fabrics. Pin and sew the side seams of these petals together to form a circle. Press seams to the side. Cut out the center piece from the main fabric and turn the edges under 1/4 inch, then baste. Applique the petals to the center of the of one of the off-white squares, then applique the circle piece to the center of the petals.

Make a quilt sandwich from the two pieces of off-white fabric and the batting, with the right sides of the fabrics facing out. Quilt the sandwich by machine or hand with the monofilament thread. From the main fabric, cut two strips measuring 7 x 44 inches (17 x 110 cm) for the ruffle. Sew the two strips together on the short side and press. Fold in half lengthwise with right sides together and sew each of the two ends. Turn and press. Sew a row of gathering stitches on the raw edge. Gather the strip to fit around the square and pin in place, allowing a 1-inch (2.5 cm) overlap where the ends meet.

For the pillow back, cut two rectangles measuring 15-1/2 x 11 inches from the main fabric. Hem one of the 15-1/2-inch sides on both rectangles as shown in the illustration. Place one of the rectangles right side down over the ruffle and position the other rectangle the same way, with the hemmed edges overlapping in the center. Stitch all around the square through all layers. Turn the pillow right sides out through the overlapped back opening. Insert foam pillow form and fluff.

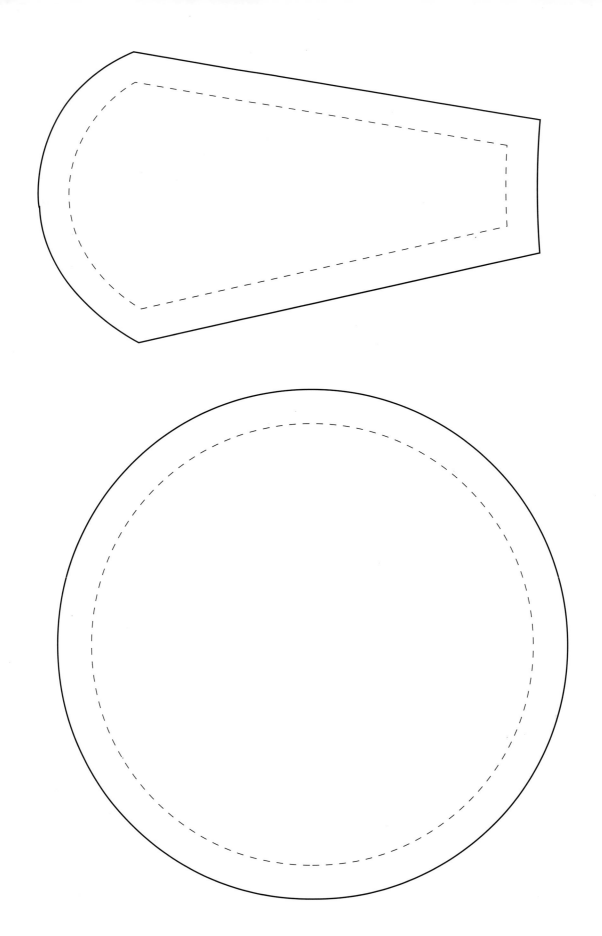

WALL HANGING

1 yard of main fabric, 1/4 yard (.2 m) of four contrasting print fabrics, 1-1/4 yards (1.1 m) of 45-inch (112 cm) quilt batting, 2 yards (1.8 m) off-white fabric for squares and back, monofilament and contrasting threads

Assemble four Dresden plate squares as you did for the pillow. Cut two strips measuring 2-1/2 x 15-1/2 inches (6.5 x 38 cm) from the main fabric and one strip measuring 2-1/2 x 32-1/2 inches (6.5 x 81 cm) from the main fabric. Assemble the borders and squares as directed in the illustration.

Cut four strips measuring 6-1/2 x 44-1/2 inches (16 x 111 cm) for the outside borders. Attach these strips to the outer edges, mitering the corners. Cut a lining 1 inch larger all the way around than the quilt top. Assemble it into a sandwich with the batting in the middle and the right sides of the fabric facing outward. Quilt as desired by hand or machine with the monofilament thread.

For hanging loops, cut four strips measuring 2-1/2 x 6 inches (6.5 x 15 cm). Fold the strips right sides together and stitch on the long edge. Turn and press. Fold them in half and pin to the top back side of the wall hanging, taking care to space them evenly. Cut four strips measuring 2-1/2 x 44 inches (6.5 x 110 cm) for the binding. Stitch the binding around all four edges. Fold under and hand stitch in place on the back side.

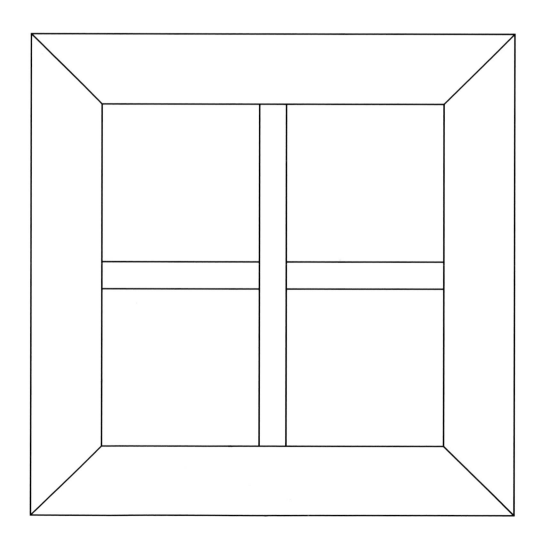

HEART WREATH

This simple heart wreath makes an ideal project to use up leftover scraps of fabric, and the wreath will emit a light fragrance if you fill some of the hearts with potpourri instead of stuffing.

 10 scraps of cotton in assorted prints and fabrics, 1-1/2 yards (1.3 m) heavy wire or unraveled coat hanger, polyester stuffing, 2-1/2 yards (2 m) blue satin ribbon, glue gun

Trace or photocopy the heart pattern. Pin the pattern onto folded fabric and cut out the hearts. Pin the hearts with their right sides facing and sew around the edges, leaving a small opening for stuffing. Trim the seams and turn right sides out. Stuff the hearts and then hand-stitch the opening closed. Repeat this process until you have approximately 50 hearts.

Shape the wire into a heart shape and secure with tape where the ends meet. Hot-glue the hearts to the wire base, positioning them at varying angles and taking care to not let any wire show. Starting at the top of the wreath, weave the ribbon down both sides and tie it in a bow at the bottom. Tack the ribbon in place if necessary.

ALL-OVER
LACE NEGLIGEE

During Victorian times, the pattern for a bridal gown was often used several times for additional dresses and a robe. For this negligee, a wedding gown pattern was modified so it opens in the front instead of the back.

 Wedding gown pattern, quantity of fabric called for in pattern (double galloon all-over lace was used here), 1 yard (.9 m) muslin (to check for pattern changes), 2 plastic snaps or small buttons

Press the lace face down on a well-padded surface with a steam iron to avoid shrinkage later, then press the muslin. (Test the iron on a corner of the lace before pressing and adjust the temperature if necessary.) Place the bodice of the pattern on the muslin. Cut out the back as indicated; note that you may need to adjust for less depth in the "V" neckline

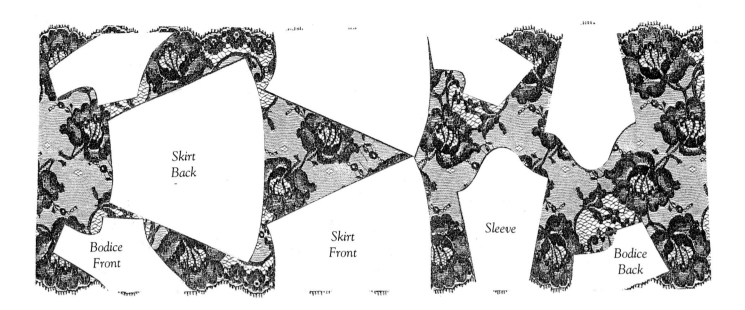

plunge. Since the negligee should open in the front instead of the back, add 1 inch (2-1/2 cm) to the center front and cut on an open edge instead of the fold. Pin back the flap of the center front neckline.

Pin the muslin together and fit on the person or a dress form. Make any needed adjustments, and then use the muslin as a bodice pattern for cutting out the lace. Lay the muslin pattern out on the right side (cordonnet side) of the lace so that the front opening of the bodice and skirt front as well as the bodice necklines are on the scalloped edge of the lace. Pin the remaining skirt front pattern pieces together. Remove enough of the back and side fullness so they will each fit on one width of the lace.

Place the back skirt pattern on the center area of the lace which has been folded right sides together. Leave the scallop edges for finishing the hem and waist. Match the lace pattern at the center back and front opening. Lay the sleeve pattern so that its hem is on the scallop. (The lace may not match at the side seam.) Cut out the lace with sharp shears. Try to follow around the lace pattern at the side seams, cutting one layer of the lace at a time. The remaining scallop border should be cut about 2-1/2 to 3 inches (6 to 7 cm) wide along the design's outline for use at the hem and waistline.

Lap the side seams, working on the right side of the lace and matching the pattern as closely as possible. Baste. Machine straight stitch along the line of the pattern match. Then stitch over the previous straight stitch line with a narrow zigzag stitch. Carefully trim away the excess side seam allowance of lace on both the front and the back. Lap the shoulder and sleeve seams, matching the lace as best as you can, but keeping in mind that the line of zigzag stitches will create a pattern line by itself. Press face down on a well-padded surface and then zigzag stitch once more over the previous stitching.

Gather the sleeves and skirt with two rows of gathering stitches. Baste the sleeves and skirt to the bodice with the right sides together. Straight stitch; then trim the seam to a 1/8-inch-width (3 mm) for the sleeves and 1/4-inch (6 mm) at the waist. Zigzag to finish the seam edges. Baste the scallop edged lace strips to the waistline and hem. Straight stitch along the pattern's design and then zigzag. Trim the edges on the front if needed. Attach clear plastic snaps or sew on small buttons and make button loops at the center front. Cut out and attach one rose or other lace design motif and stitch between the "V" at the center back of the bodice.

QUILTED
APPLIQUÉ DRESS

This simple jumper dress makes a fun project to experiment with machine quilting. If these motifs aren't suited to your gift recipient, create your own motifs by cutting out shapes and patterns from magazines.

Purchased jumper pattern with a lined top, amount of fabrics called for in your pattern's instructions, 1 yard (.9 m) fleece, scraps of contrasting fabric for appliqué, iron-on webbing, freezer paper

Cut out the jumper as directed in the pattern instructions. Cut out a piece of fleece using the top back and front pattern pieces. Baste the fleece to the wrong side of the top front and back fabrics, and then assemble the top portion of the dress as directed. Press well.

Machine or hand quilt the top of the dress in the pattern of your choice. Cut out three dogwood blooms, five leaves, and the stems. Then cut out the shapes in iron-on webbing. Attach the webbing to the back of the appliqués, following the manufacturer's instructions. Arrange the motifs on the front of the jumper and iron them in place.

Iron a square of freezer paper, shiny side down, against the fabric that's behind the appliqué. (The freezer paper will make the fabric smoother and flatter as you sew.) Satin stitch around the outside of the flower petals and leaves, and then satin stitch the middle lines. Tear the freezer paper away from the back of the jumper top.

Sew the lining and the top of the jumper together as directed in the pattern. Using monofilament thread on top and a fine cotton thread on the bobbin, machine quilt on the front and back of the top. Attach the top to the jumper skirt as directed in the pattern, and hem.

HAND TOWEL

This simple project lets you customize an inexpensive towel to match the gift recipient's bathroom, and takes just an afternoon to make.

White hand towel, worsted-weight cotton yarn in four colors, disappearing fabric marker, embroidery needle

Measure a sewing guide line 4 inches (10 cm) up from the bottom of the towel and mark it with the fabric marker. Stitch the first row of embroidery on top of this line using a simple running stitch in a gauge that feels comfortable to you. Create the next three rows each in a different color, using each preceding first row as a guide for the next row.

QUILT FAN
PLACE MATS

Choosing fabrics with rich tones and lush
patterns for these place mats often ties the look
of an entire room together, and you may well
choose to leave them on your dining table all the
time. Before you go shopping, check your fabric
stashes to be sure you don't already have enough
scraps in compatible colors and patterns.

For Four Place Mats: 1/2 yard (.45 m) of four different fabrics, 1 yard (.9 m) extra of one of the four fabrics or of a fifth color for the place mat backs, 1 yard fleece, nylon (optional) and matching threads

Fold the fabric selvage to selvage with right sides together, then fold again with the fold to the selvage. From fabric one, cut out patterns D and B eight times. From fabric two, cut out patterns D and B eight times. From fabric three, cut out patterns C and A eight times. From fabric four, cut out patterns C

and A eight times. Cut four center circles from the fabric of your choice. Cut four rectangles measuring 22 x 17 inches (56 x 43 cm) from the fleece and four from the backing fabric.

Pin one of each color of the D pieces together and sew, beginning at the top outside curve 1/4 inch (6 mm) from the top and sewing all the way down to the narrow end. (Refer to the illustration as a piecing guide.) Repeat the above process with the A pieces. Arrange all of the sewn and unsewn pieces face-up on a flat surface and match their positions to the diagrams. You will have two place mats laid out like diagram A and two like diagram B.

Pin all the pieces with right sides together and sew, beginning 1/4 inch from the outside curve and sewing all the way to the center. Press the seams open.

Place the backing fabric right side up on top of the fleece and then place the pieced fan right side down on top of the backing fabric. Sew a 1/4-inch seam all the way around the place mat's outer edge. Trim away any excess fabric and fleece and clip at the seams. Turn the place mat right side out through the center, making sure that all of the curves are pushed out smooth.

Press each place mat well and press a 1/4-inch hem around the outside edges of the four circles. Line the circles up over the center of each place mat and blindstitch them in place. Machine or hand quilt as you like. The place mats shown here were decorated with ditch stitching on the fan and in an allover pattern on the circle. Note: For machine quilting, place the nylon thread on the spool and the matching color thread in the bobbin.

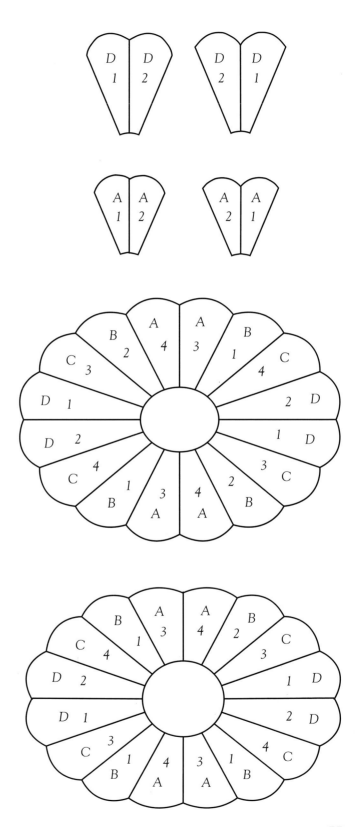

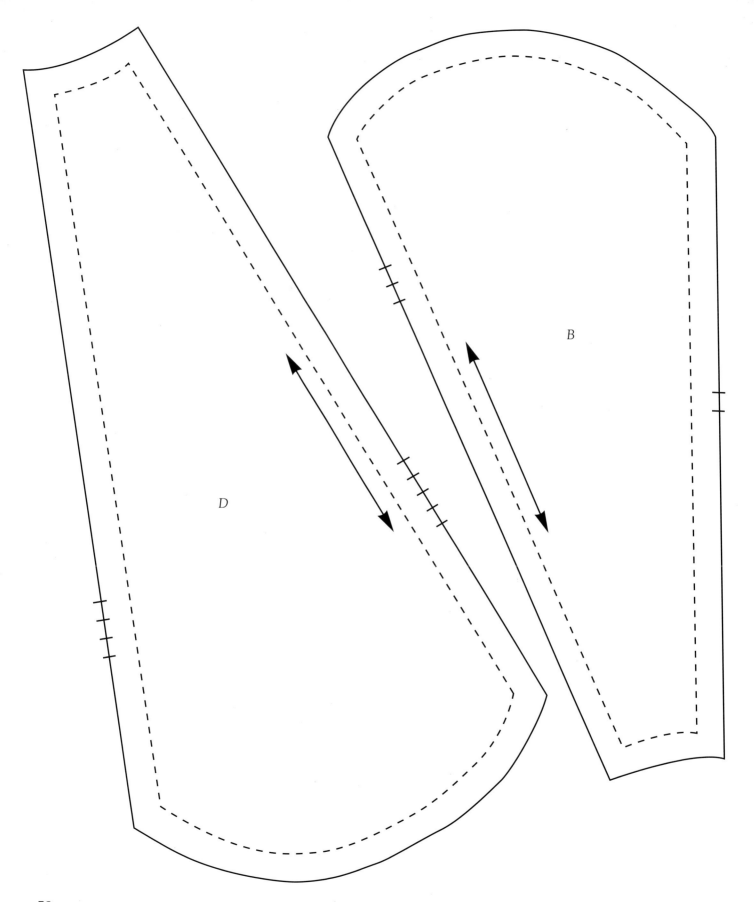

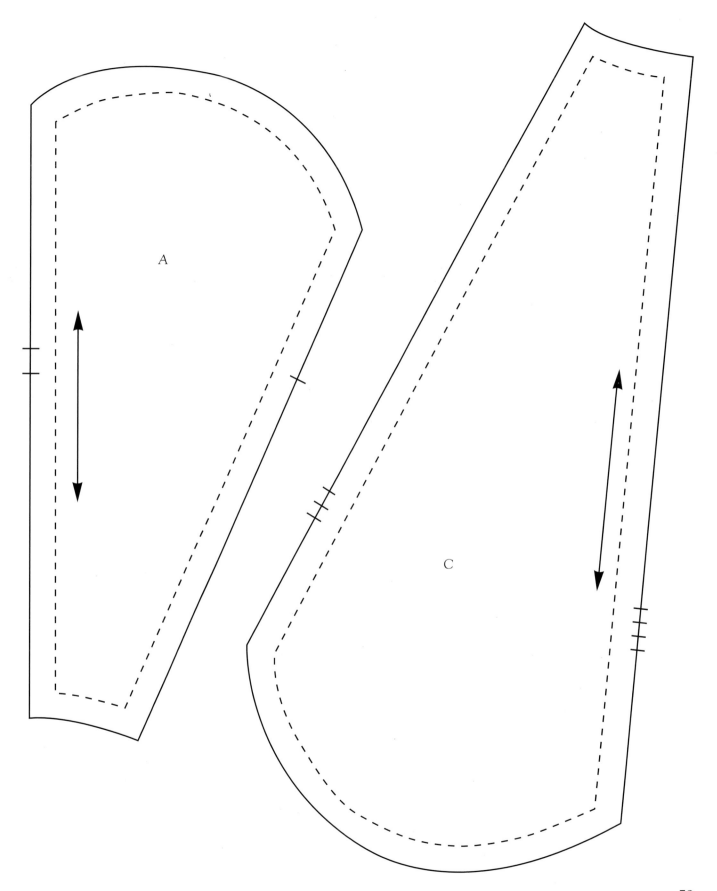

A

C

FABRIC CAKE

This fun fabric confection takes just a few scraps of felt and makes a festive decoration for parties and everyday use.

 Small squares of beige, brown, white, and red felt, a red wooden ball, pink and brown embroidery floss, stuffing

Cut out the pattern pieces for the cake's top and bottom from red and brown felt. Cut out the rounded piece from the white felt. For the sides of the cake, cut out two rectangles measuring 3-1/2 x 5-1/2 inches (9 x 14 cm) from the beige felt. For the back of the cake, cut out a 3-1/2-inch (9 cm) square piece of brown felt.

Using the photo as a guide, embroider the icing lines between the layers in pink and brown in a satin stitch. Sew the pieces together with right sides facing, leaving a small opening for stuffing. Turn right sides out, stuff, and hand sew the opening closed. Sew a row of gathering stitches around the edges of the white felt, adjust the stitches to fit the top of the cake, and then sew it to the top of the cake for the whipped cream. Last, hot-glue the wooden ball in place for the cherry.

Pattern on page 85

CHRISTMAS ANGEL

Angels have long been a traditional part of holiday celebrations, holding the symbolic position of the messenger of peace and good will. The gown for this angel is styled like one England's Queen Victoria might have worn during the early years of her reign in the 1840s.

 Young girl doll, 11-1/2 inches (28 cm) tall, 1/3 yard (.3 m) gold metallic fabric, 1 yard (.9 m) medium-weight iron-on interfacing, 1/3 yard white all-over pattern lace, 3 yards (2.7 m) white lace flounce/edging, about 2-1/2 inches (6 cm) wide, 2 yards (1.8 m) narrow white lace edging, 4 pieces of 18-inch (46 cm) white floral wire, wire cutters, gold glitter, glue gun, white floral tape

Press the interfacing to the back of the gold metallic fabric, taking care not to wrinkle the fabric. (Test a small corner first and adjust the iron's temperature if necessary.) Place the all-over lace on top of the gold metallic fabric. Pin the pattern to the folded lace and the fabric with the center front of both the skirt and the bodice/sleeve sections placed on the fold. Cut out one skirt and one bodice.

To form the wings, first cut out a 9- x 11-inch (22 x 27 cm) rectangle of all-over lace. Place a piece of aluminum foil on your work surface to protect it from glue spills and place a piece of plastic wrap on top of the foil. (The lace wings may stick to the plastic, but it can be easily torn away after they dry.)

Form the fabric-covered wire into the pattern's wing shape, joining at the center back. Place them on top of the lace rectangle. Glue the edges of the wire to the lace, and set aside to dry. (You can stitch the lace to the wire instead of gluing if desired.)

To form the bodice and sleeves, stitch the lace to the gold metallic fabric, starting at the neckline. Turn a 1/8-inch (3 mm) hem to the outside at the neckline and finger press. Sew the bodice side/sleeve seams and press open. Turn a 5/8-inch (15 mm) hem toward the inside of the sleeves and glue in place.

Set the lace skirt aside. Stitch the back seam of the gold metallic underskirt, leaving an opening at the top. Press. Zig-zag around the lower edge of the underskirt. Press a 1/4-inch (6 mm) hem to the inside of the skirt and stitch with yellow thread. (Glue may be used here instead of sewing.)

Match the pattern of about 2-1/2 yards (2.3 m) of the white lace flounce. Overlap the ends and zigzag stitch them together. Replace the yellow thread with white. Gather and pin the flounce to the gold metallic underskirt about 2 inches (5 cm) above the lower edge, allowing a little of the lace edge to extend beyond the hem of the skirt. Straight stitch in place.

Gather the narrow lace edging and attach it to the lower edge of the lace overskirt. Gather the overskirt from the hem to the waist at the back opening. Pull the threads tight and tack at the waist. Gather the remaining lace flounce and stitch it to the neckline of the bodice. Gather up half the depth of the skirt from the hem at the center front and both side fronts. Pull up and attach a gold rose to each point on the skirt and at the neckline front.

Place the lace overskirt on top of the gold underskirt and gather together at the waist. Attach it to the bodice and finish the seam with a zigzag stitch. Trim the lace close to the wire on the wing shape. Spread the glue along the wire edge of the wings for about 2 inches. Sprinkle or dip the wings into gold glitter. Continue working a little at a time until the edges of the wings are completely covered with glitter. Set aside to dry.

Form the halo by twisting a length of white floral wire around the waist of the undressed doll. Make a circle 2 inches in diameter at one end of the other piece of the wire. Spread glue around the circle (halo), and dip it in the glitter. Join the other end of the halo wire to the wire around the doll's waist. Wrap the wire rising from the waist to the halo with the white tape. Dress the doll. Close the back seam of her gown with the wire protruding from the waist. Handstitch the back seam closed. Glue the center of the wings to the halo's wire at shoulder height.

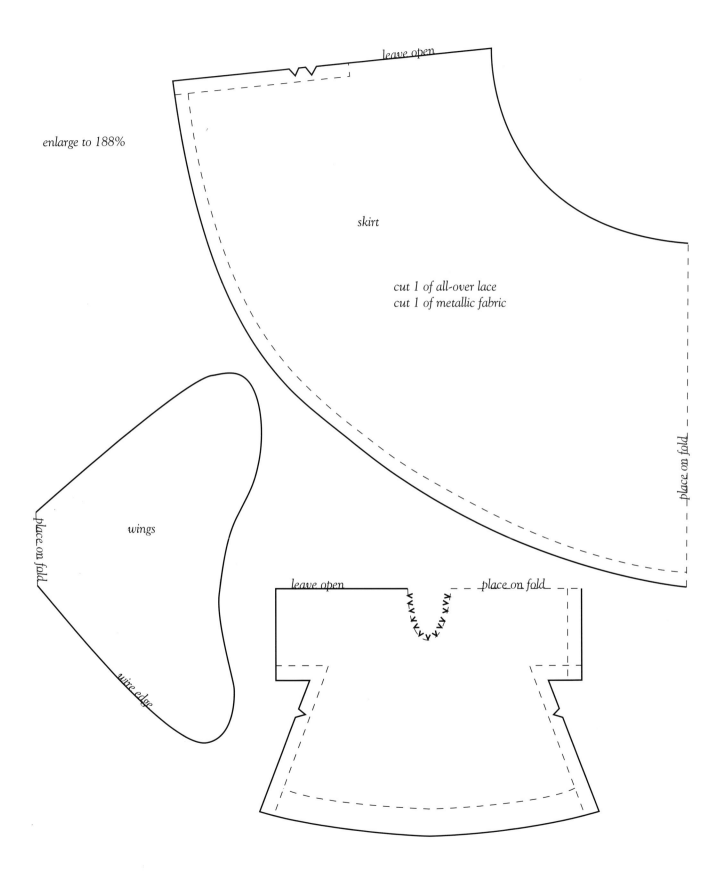

leave open

enlarge to 188%

skirt

cut 1 of all-over lace
cut 1 of metallic fabric

place on fold

wings

place on fold

wire edge

leave open

place on fold

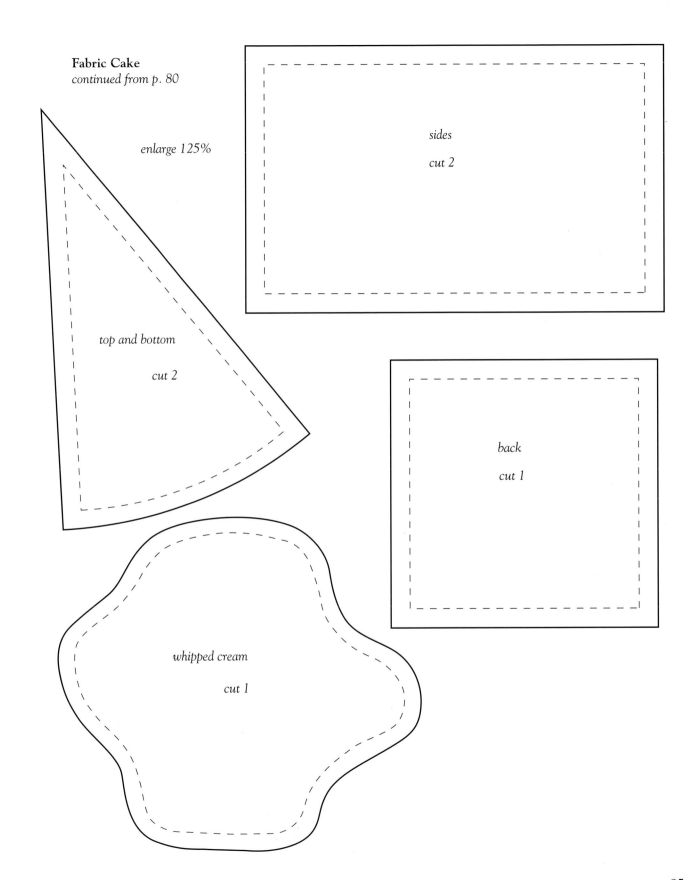

Fabric Cake
continued from p. 80

enlarge 125%

sides

cut 2

top and bottom

cut 2

back

cut 1

whipped cream

cut 1

CHILDREN'S CURIOSITIES

OF ALL THE GOOD REASONS TO SEW GIFTS FOR CHILDREN, NONE CAN COMPARE WITH THAT MOST DREADED OF GIFT-FINDING ALTERNATIVES: THE TOY STORE. FIFTEEN MINUTES IN ANY LARGE TOY STORE CAN RAISE STRESS LEVELS HIGHER THAN A TAX AUDIT. IS THE ITEM AGE APPROPRIATE? WILL IT FALL APART IN A WEEK? ARE THERE PARTS THAT A SMALLER SIBLING COULD CHOKE ON? AH, HAPPY THE SEWER WHO CAN REACH INTO A BOX OF FABRIC SCRAPS AND WHIP UP A GIFT. THE PROJECTS IN THIS CHAPTER VARY FROM SIMPLE TRINKETS, SUCH AS THE MINI-TEDDYS AND PENCIL CARRIERS, TO GIFTS SUCH AS THE FOLD-UP PILLOW QUILT THAT WILL BE ENJOYED FOR YEARS TO COME.

COAT HANGER

Designed to hang a special outfit such as christening dress, this fabric hanger makes a useful gift to celebrate a birth. Decorative hangers can also be made for adults by adding enough extra width and length to fit the larger size hanger. For a fragrant touch, sprigs of dried lavender or rose petals can be mixed in with the padding.

Child's size coat hanger (plastic or wooden), narrow satin ribbon, 1/4 yard (.2 m) each pink and white cotton fabric (or suitable alternative colors), quilt batting, glue gun

Tightly wrap the narrow ribbon around the hanger's hook, beginning at the end of the hook and ending where the hook meets the body of the hanger. Secure the ribbon ends with a dab of hot glue if necessary.

Cut five strips measuring 1 inch wide x 5 inches long (2.5 x 13 cm) from the white fabric and four from the pink. Cut two strips of pink measuring 4 inches wide x 5 inches long (10 x 13 cm). Using the photos as a guide, stitch the strips together. Press all seams open.

Fold the pieced fabric in half lengthwise and mark the center with a pin. Unfold the fabric and stitch a buttonhole at the center mark. Pad the body of the hanger with quilt batting, and then gently insert the hanger's hook through the buttonhole.

Allowing for some ease, mark the excess fabric areas on the edges. Remove the fabric and press the fabric under as indicated by the pins. Handstitch a row of gathering stitches on each short end and place the fabric back on the hanger. Gently gather the end fabrics and tack in place, then whipstitch the long edges together.

COUNTRY GIRL
PILLOWS

This lovely gift set will be adored by parent and child alike: the parents will enjoy the way the projects dress up a child's room, while the child will adore snuggling under her quilt and then folding it into a pillow.

PILLOW

1 yard (.9 m) main fabric (for ruffle and back), scrap of contrasting fabric, 2 15-1/2-inch (41 cm) squares of off-white fabric, 15-1/2-inch square quilt batting, 14-inch (36 cm) pillow form, monofilament and matching threads

Cut out the country doll's dress and arm from the main fabric, and cut out the hat, one hand, and two shoes from the contrasting fabric. Position the doll on top of one of the off-white fabric squares and machine appliqué in place.

Make a sandwich from the two pieces of off-white fabric and the batting, with the right sides of the fabrics facing out and the batting in the middle. Quilt the sandwich by machine or hand with the monofilament thread. From the main fabric, cut two strips measuring 7 x 44 inches (17 x 110 cm) for the ruffle. Sew the short side of the the two strips together with right sides facing and press. Fold in half lengthwise with right sides together and sew each of the two ends. Turn and press. Sew a row of gathering stitches on the raw edge. Gather the edge to fit around the square and pin in place, allowing a 1-inch (2.5 cm) overlap where the ends meet.

For the pillow back, cut two rectangles measuring 15-1/2 x 11 inches (41 x 27 cm) from the main fabric. Hem one of the 15-1/2-inch sides on both rectangles as shown in the illustration. Place one of the rectangles right side down over the ruffle and place the other rectangle the same way, with the hemmed edges overlapping in the center. Stitch all around the square through all layers. Turn the pillow right sides out through the overlapped back opening. Insert the foam pillow form and fluff.

Quilt

2-1/4 yards (2.1 m) of main fabric, 2-1/2 yards (2.3 m) contrasting print fabric, 2-1/2 yards of 45-inch quilt batting, 1 15-1/2-inch square off-white fabric, monofilament and matching threads

Appliqué a country girl square as you did for the pillow. Assemble a sandwich with the batting on the bottom, a 15-1/2-inch square of the contrasting fabric with its right side facing up in the center, and the appliquéd square facing right side down on the top. Sew around three edges, leaving the top edge open. Turn right sides out.

Cut one rectangle measuring 72 x 44 inches (165 x 110) from the main fabric, and one from the contrasting fabric and one from the batting. Assemble a sandwich with the batting on the bottom, the contrasting rectangle with right side facing up in the middle, and the appliqué square with its right side facing down and its raw edge centered on the 44-inch side on the top. Place the main color rectangle right side down on top of the others. Pin all the layers in place. Stitch on all sides, leaving an 8-inch (20 cm) opening on the bottom 44-inch side for turning. Turn right sides out and press well. Quilt the large rectangle by hand or machine in the pattern of your choice.

Bring the little pillow down onto the rectangle with its appliqué side facing down and stitch the two outside edges of the appliquéd square through all the layers of the rectangle. Fold the quilt into a pillow, using the illustration as a guide.

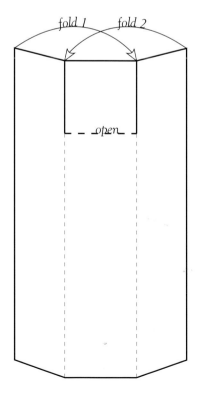

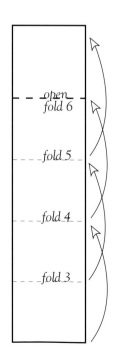

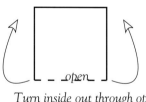

Turn inside out through open end

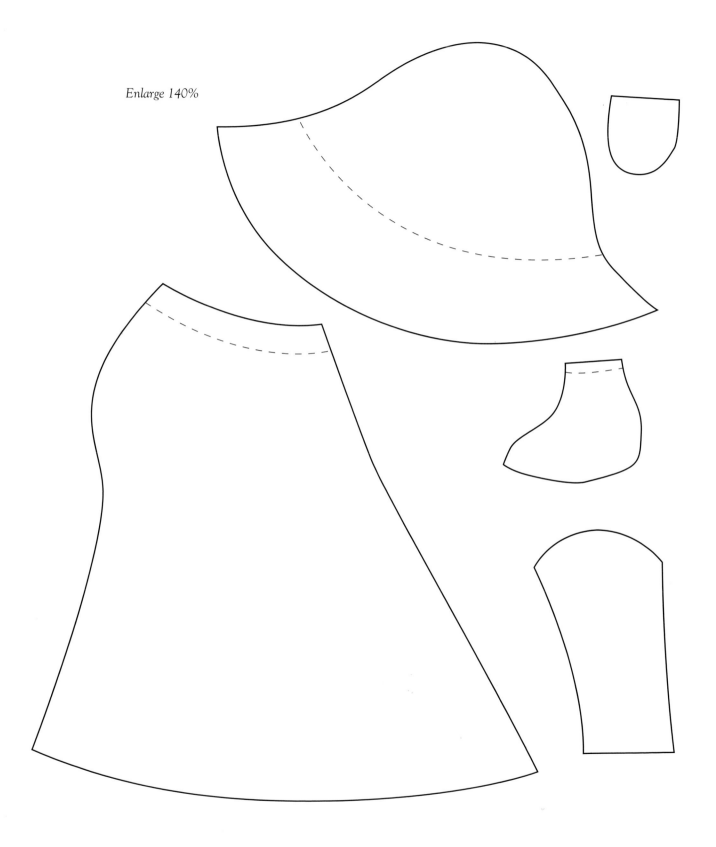

Enlarge 140%

93

FESTIVE BEACH TOWELS

These fun appliqué projects are sure to be a hit at the beach, and the designs can be adapted to suit your gift recipient.

 1 yard (.9 m) muslin (for swimmer towel), 1 yard red or green terry cloth (for frog towel), 1 yard of a colored terry cloth for the backing for each towel, 1 yard of terry cloth in the colors indicated on the chart for each towel, 1 additional yard of terry for border strips for each towel, 1 yard of quilt batting for each towel

Swimmer and Frog: Cut out an appliqué background piece measuring 24-3/4 x 36-3/4 inches (62 x 92 cm) from the white muslin for the swimmer towel, and a background piece of red terry cloth with the same measurements for the frog towel. Add a 4-1/4-inch (11 cm) border on all sides of both towels.

Enlarge the appliqué patterns on a photocopier and cut them out, adding seam allowances on the outside edges and no seam allowances where the pieces will be zigzagged together. Baste the appliqué pieces onto each background and sew in place with contrasting thread. Embroider the facial features in a contrasting color, and then zigzag along the outer edges of all the pieces. Remove the basting stitches.

Using the appliquéd towel fronts as a pattern, cut out a piece of batting and a piece of backing fabric for each towel. Pin the batting to the wrong side of the towel. Sew the back and front pieces with their right sides facing, leaving an opening for turning. Turn right sides out and hand stitch the opening closed. Zigzag along the appliquéd square and along the diagonal corners. Sew horizontal and vertical lines through the background of all three thicknesses with contrasting thread, intersecting the lines every 1-1/4 inches (3 cm) on the swimmer towel and every 1/2 inch (12 mm) on the frog towel.

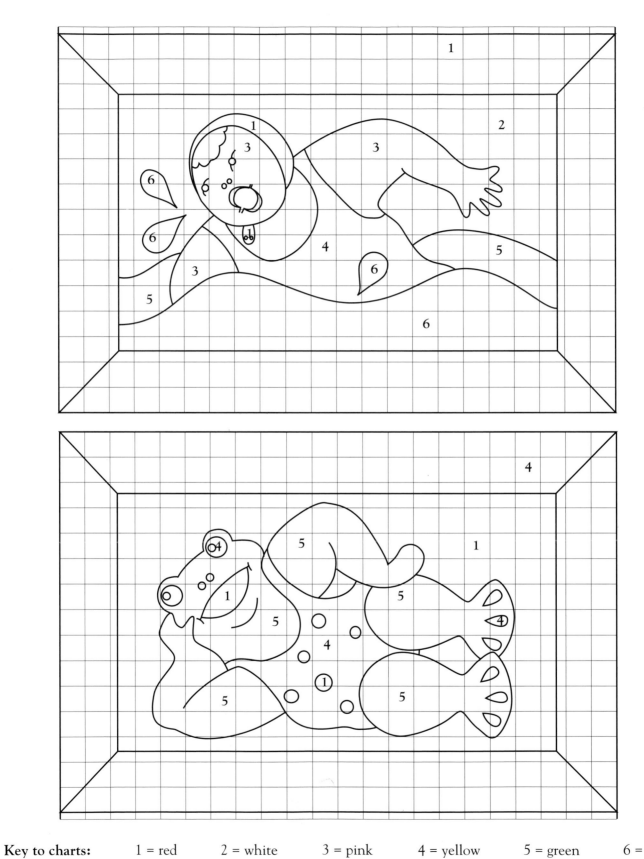

Key to charts: 1 = red   2 = white   3 = pink   4 = yellow   5 = green   6 = blue

96

FABRIC BASSINET

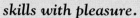

This portable bassinet makes a welcome gift for a child and his or her special companion. The bassinet's accessories — a pillow and a cover sheet — let children practice their parenting skills with pleasure.

3/4 yard (.7 m) cotton print fabric, 1/2 yard (.45 m) corduroy, 1/2 yard fusible interfacing, 1/2 yard quilt batting, contrasting color of cording

For the bassinet, enlarge the pattern to 400% cut out one from the batting, one from the print fabric, one from the corduroy, and one from the interfacing. Also cut out two strips measuring 3-1/2 x 12-1/2 inches (9 x 31 cm) for the handles and a 1-1/2-inch (4 cm) bias strip from the print fabric.

Iron the interfacing to the back of the corduroy. Stitch the side seams of the corduroy and then stitch the side seams of the print fabric. Trim the seams and turn both pieces right sides out. Pin the batting as though you were going to sew the side seams. Trim the excess fabric, remove the pins, and arrange the batting inside the corduroy form.

Place the print bassinet form on top of the quilt batting, and baste all three layers together around the top. Fold one of the long edges of the bias strip down 1/4 inch (6 mm) and top stitch. Pin the cording about 1/2 inch (12 mm) down from the top and then pin the unsewn edge of the bias strip all the way around with right sides facing. Remove the cording pins and stitch. Trim the seam, fold the bias strip halfway over, and whipstitch it to the inside of the bassinet.

With right sides facing, stitch the long edges of the handle strips. Turn right sides out and lightly press the short edges under 1/4 inch. Position the handles about 1 inch (2.5 cm) down on the inside of the bassinet and handstitch in place.

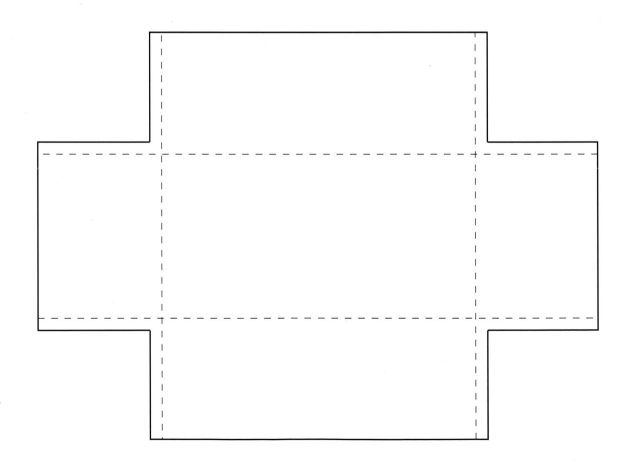

For the pillow, cut out a rectangle measuring 6-1/2 x 10 inches (16 x 25 cm) from the print fabric. Fold in half widthwise with right sides facing and stitch, leaving a small opening for turning. Turn right sides out, press, and stuff with quilt batting. Handstitch the opening closed. For the cover sheet, hem a 14- x 13-inch (36 x 33 cm) piece of the print fabric on all sides.

ANIMAL BAGS

These adorable versions of the traditional pencil bag can be used to carry pencils, erasers, lunch money, etc. to school, or just to hide cherished possessions. The outside of the dogs can be decorated with one or more surface design techniques, or you can allow the child to decorate the dog by him/herself.

1/4 yard (.2 m) sturdy fabric, sew-on or adhesive Velcro, scraps of fabric in assorted colors, fabric glue, fabric paint (optional)

Enlarge the pattern and cut out two dogs. Sew around the entire body, leaving the flat, back seam open. Clip the seams, turn, and press. Press the back seam down 1/4 inch (6 mm) and fit one length of Velcro on each edge. Decorate the outside of the dog with fabric paint and/or by gluing on small shapes of fabric.

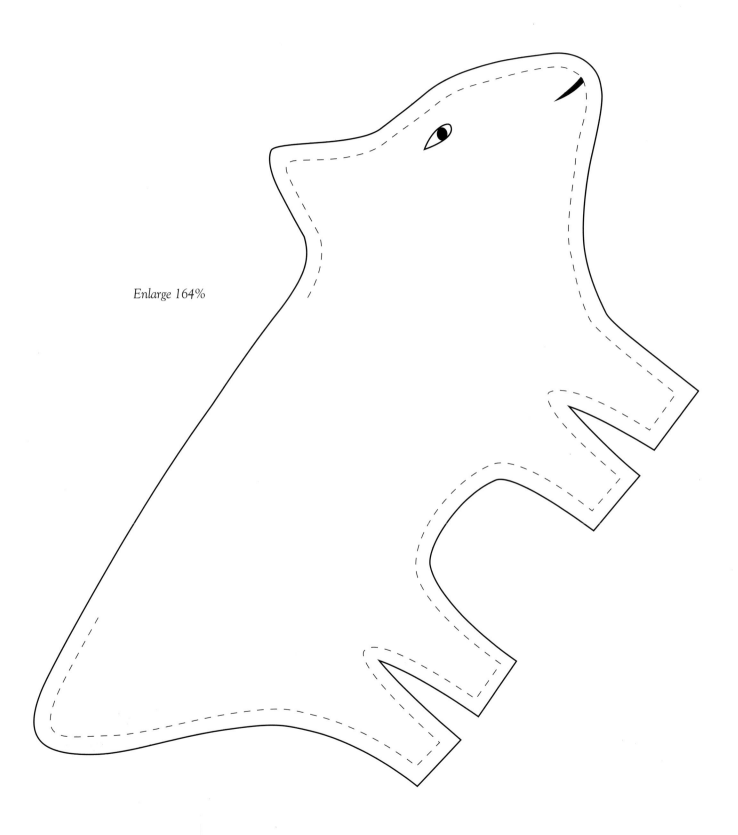

Enlarge 164%

CLOWN

This charming clown adds a playful touch to any child's room and its versatile stomach pouch can be filled with diapers, mittens, or any other lightweight objects.

1-1/2 yards (1.35 m) black or dark-colored felt, scraps of felt in seven different colors, three red buttons, fabric glue, wooden hanger, glue gun

Attach the colored felt pieces to the clown with fabric glue. Topstitch around the outer edges. Make three buttonholes and sew on the buttons. Hot-glue the clown's fingers to the hanger.

Enlarge the patterns to 3 feet (.9 m) in height. Cut out the back and front of the clown's body from the black felt, then cut out the colored felt shapes. Stitch the stomach seam 1 inch (2.5 cm) down from the top and then stitch 1 inch up from the bottom. With right sides facing, pin and stitch around the outside of the clown's body and turn right sides out through the stomach.

BABY SEATS

These lightweight baby seats fit around virtually any chair to provide stability for visiting babies. The seats take less than an afternoon to sew and make great gifts for both the parents and grandparents of young children.

1 yard (.9 m) of quilted double-sided print fabric, bias cut strips or commercial binding in a contrasting solid color

Using the illustration as a guide, cut out one apron from the print fabric.

Fold the wider edge up 11 inches (28 cm) with right sides facing and sew both side seams. Turn right sides out and press. Bind all of the edges with the bias strips or the binding, saving the narrow straight edge for last. Allow about 3 feet (.9 m) of binding to protrude on each end of the narrow edge to serve as ties.

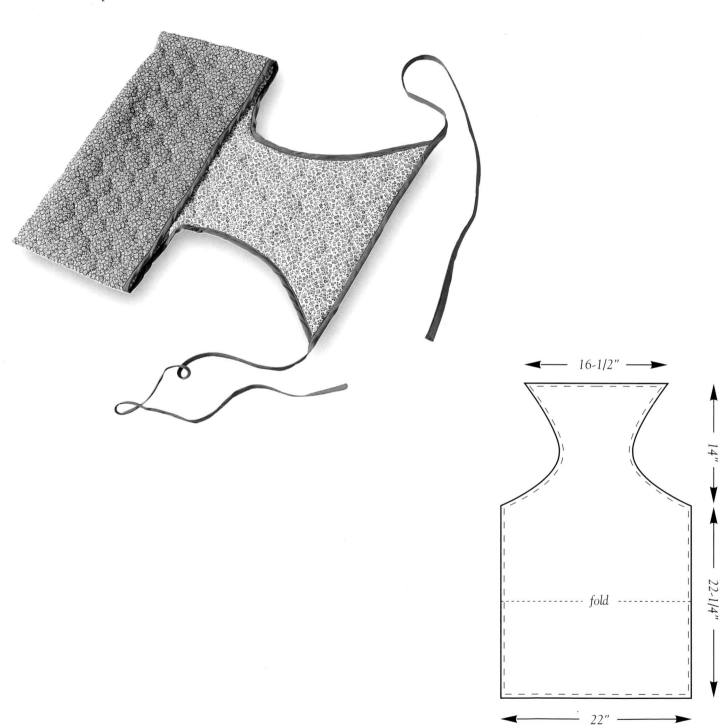

16-1/2"

14"

22-1/4"

fold

22"

KITCHEN INSPIRATIONS

This colorful collection of kitchen wear is sure to inspire young chefs in all their culinary creations. The decorative motifs were inspired by the shapes of cookie cutters.

CHEF HAT

 2/3 yard (.6 m) heavy fabric, scraps of fabric in bright colors, 1/8 yard (.1 m) heavy fleece, 2/3 yard multicolored woven fabric ribbon

Cut out a rectangle measuring 10 x 20 inches (25 x 50 cm) from the heavy fabric. Fold the rectangle in half to form a square with right sides together and sew the side seam down 2 inches. Sew gathering stitches on the narrow end adjacent to the sewn seam. Cut out the circle from the fabric scraps. Fold the edges of the circle under and baste. Gather the narrow end whose side seam has been sewn until you have a circle about 2 inches in diameter. Tie off the gathering threads. Position the circle over the center of the gathered circle, baste in place, and topstitch.

Cut one band from fabric and one band from the fleece that's 5 inches wide and 1-1/2 inches (4 cm) longer than the distance around the intended wearer's head. Baste the fleece to the wrong side of the fabric, then stitch the band together on the short ends with a 1/2-inch seam. Press and turn right sides out.

Sew the remainder of the square's side seam. Sew a row of gathering stitches around the bottom edge and gather to fit the band. Sew one edge of the band to the hat and press the seam down toward the band. Cut out and applique the motifs to the band. Press the bottom edge of the band under 1/2 inch. Fold the band under and whipstitch in place near the seam. Last, topstitch the ribbon in place.

MITT

 1/3 yard (.3 m) heavy fabric, 1/3 yard heavy fleece, scraps of fabric in bright colors, 1 package of bias binding

Cut four mitts from the fabric and two from the fleece on folded fabric. Cut out the applique shapes and attach them to the mitts. Place one mitt wrong side up. Place fleece on top of it then place another mitt wrong side down on top of the fleece. Sew the binding across the wrist edge of the mitt. Repeat with the other mitts and the fleece. Place the two mitts together with the appliques facing out. Pin and baste on all sides except the wrist side. Sew the binding around these same edges.

APRON

1 yard (.9 m) durable fabric, 1 package of matching bias binding, 2 yards (1.8 m) multicolored woven fabric ribbon, fabric scraps in several bright colors, scrap of fabric in a neutral color

Cut the apron as shown in the diagram. cut two pockets measuring 7 x 10 inches (18 x 25 cm). Turn the pockets under 1/2 inch (12 mm) on all sides, then turn down 2 inches (5 cm) at the tops and top-stitch. Place a pocket on each side of the apron, pin, and topstitch in place. Sew the bias binding around all edges of the apron. Sew the neck and waist ties in place.

Cut out the cookie cutter shapes and appliqué them to the apron. For the rolling pin appliqué, cut out six strips of fabric measuring 2 x 4 inches (5 x 10 cm). Sew the strips together on their short ends and press the seams open. Press all the edges down 1/4 inch (6 mm) and pin in place. Cut out the rolling pin handles from the neutral fabric and press the edges down. Pin the handles in place, placing the edges that butt against the pin under the short edges of the rolling pin. Appliqué the rolling pin in place.

Enlarge 150%

POCKET
TEDDY BEARS

These simple bears can be enjoyed in any number of ways: thread a metal loop onto the ribbon for a key chain; fill them with potpourri to add fragrance to a baby nursery; decorate a Christmas tree with teddy bears; or stash them in the glove box to amuse bored children on a long car ride. For added amusement, place a musical button, available in craft stores, inside the bear before stuffing.

 Scraps of fabric in assorted colors, narrow satin ribbon, stuffing material

For Each Bear: Cut out the bear pattern from doubled fabric and sew the two pieces together with right sides facing, leaving a small opening on one side for turning. Trim the seams and turn right sides out, using the points of your scissors to press out any fabric that doesn't want to turn.

Fold a 3-inch (7.5 cm) length of narrow ribbon in half and tack the bottom edges to the back side of the bear. Decorate the bear with a bow around the neck and/or a vest.

MICE

These cuddly, adorable mice are machine washable and are light enough to send through the mail without a special occasion, just to say "I'm thinking of you."

 Materials for One Mouse: 1/2 yard (.45 m) blue terry cloth, scraps of red and white felt, embroidery floss, stuffing
Materials for Mouse Clothing: Scraps of print fabric, two 20-inch (50 cm) lengths of bias strips 1-1/4 inches (3 cm) wide, narrow elastic

Cut out the patterns for the ears and body from doubled fabric. Pin the pieces right sides together. Stitch the top body together with a 1/4-inch (6 mm) seam, leaving a small opening in the head for turning. Trim any excess seam allowance. Turn right sides out, stuff, and hand stitch the opening closed.

Embroider a red circle in a chain stitch on the front of each ear. Place the ears right sides together and sew around the edges, leaving a small opening for turning. Turn right sides out, stuff, and sew the top of the ears in place on top of the head. Cut out eyes, a nose, and a mouth from the felt scraps and sew with small stitches in matching thread. Make eyebrows and whiskers as shown in the photo.

For the pinnafore, cut out two pieces from doubled print fabric from the patterns. Sew the center front and back seams. Gather the top edge to 3-1/4 inches and sew it to the top piece, then sew the sides of the top pieces with their right sides together. Fold the top edge to the inside and slip stitch in place. Fold the bias edging around the armholes, leaving 8-inch (20 cm) ends at the top. Sew in place, then hem the remaining edges.

(Pattern on page 122)

ABC BED SET

This custom bed set is sure to make children feel special as they snuggle down under the covers. Matching curtains, dust ruffles, and table top covers can be also be made, and the letter patterns can be reduced or enlarged on a sizing photocopier if different sizes are desired.

BEDSPREAD

2 yards (1.8 m) checked cotton 60 inches (1.5 m) wide, 2 yards quilt batting, scraps of bright cotton in several colors, fusible interfacing

Cut out two rectangles measuring 60 x 47 inches (150 x 118 cm) from the fabric and two from the batting. Loosely baste one piece of batting to the wrong side of each of the fabric pieces. Enlarge the letter patterns on a photocopying machine until you're happy with their size. Cut out the desired letters from the fabric scraps and the interfacing, using the graph as a guide. Join the letters to the interfacing, then zigzag them to the front of the bedspread cover in a diagonal line, using the photo as a guide.

With right sides facing, pin all four edges together, leaving a 20-inch (50 cm) opening for turning on the bottom edge. Carefully stitch the edges with a 5/8-inch (14 mm) seam, watching to make sure that the batting does not slip out of the seam. Turn right sides out and slipstitch the opening closed. The spread can be machine quilted at this point or used as is.

PILLOW CASE

3/4 yard (.6 m) checked cotton 60 inches (1.5 m) wide, scraps of bright cotton in several colors, fusible interfacing

With the narrow edge on the fold, cut out a rectangle measuring 20 x 28 inches from doubled fabric. Enlarge the lettern patterns on a photocopying machine. Cut out the desired letters from the fabric scraps and the

interfacing. Join the letters to the interfacing, then zigzag them to the front of the pillow cover in a diagonal line, using the photo as a guide.

Sew the two sides seams together with right sides facing. Turn and press. Press the raw edge under 1/4 inch (6 mm), then press under another inch (2.5 cm). Topstitch the hem in place.

ABCDEF
GHIJKL
MNOPQ
RSTUV
WXYZ

ABCDEF
GHIJKL
MNOPQ
RSTUV
WXYZ

Mice
continued from page 118

Enlarge 210%

APPENDIX OF BASIC SEWING TECHNIQUES

Below is a quick review of some of the techniques used in this book. If you're having difficulty, remember that virtually every stitch can be pulled out, so no mistake is unfixable.

Seam Trimming — Seams are usually trimmed to eliminate excess bulk and make turning easier. It's especially important to trim seams when using heavy fabrics. In this book, the instructions will call for trimming when it's needed. Be careful not to trim closer than 1/4 inch away from the seam to prevent unraveling.

Curved Seams — Curves are a challenge for even experienced sewers, probably because it's just so much fun speeding along that anything forcing you to slow down poses a challenge. The key is to work slowly and gently guide the fabric where you want it to go. Sometimes you may need to stop the machine, lift the presser foot with the needle through the fabric, and turn the fabric in the correct direction. To make turning easier and to make the seam pressable, make several clips into curved seams.

Basting Stitches — Basting stitches are loose stitches that can easily be pulled later without harming the fabric. It doesn't matter how neatly you sew or what color thread you use — in fact, sometimes it's easier to use a totally incompatible color for basting stitches because then it's so easy to see them when it comes time for removal. Most basting stitches are just simple running stitches. They are usually done by hand, since you tend to have more control by hand than with a machine. Use basting for hard-to-sew corners, when working with a fabric that wants to slip out from under the presser foot, to check the fit of a garment, or just when you want more control.

Bias Tape Binding —

Creates a nicely finished seam that won't stretch or unravel. First, place the right side of the binding against the wrong side of the fabric with the raw edges even. Sew the binding in place and press the seam toward the binding. Next, turn the binding's folded edge to the item's right side to encase the raw edge. Press, then stitch close to the fold.

Bias Strips —

Bias strips can be made at home to use in place of store-bought bias tape binding. The strips are cut on the bias because fabric cut on this angle has more natural "give" to it. To cut your own strips, place a single layer of pressed fabric on a flat surface and begin cutting from one corner across the diagonal to the other. Continue cutting strips from the fabric to the left and to the right of your first cut. The strips should be about an inch wide, and can be stitched together to form the desired length.

Gathering Stitches — Gathering stitches are used to evenly distribute excess fabric when one of the two fabrics in a seam is longer than the other. Sometimes, as with a sleeve cap, the difference in length is minimal, and gathers are used to add ease. Other times, such as when working with a ruffle, one length of fabric may be twice as long as the other.

To make gathering stitches, first set the stitch length to its longest setting and stitch two rows about 1/4 inch from each other, the first one on the seam allowance measurement and the second one 1/4 inch closer to the fabric's edge. To gather, gently pull the top or bottom threads, taking care to pull them evenly so both rows of stitches receive even tension. To gather long areas, divide both lengths of fabric into several sections and mark them with pins, then just gather until the pins match.

Slipstitching
(also known as
Blindstitching) —
This stitch is used
when you need to
secure several layers
together with the
stitches invisible on
both sides. In this

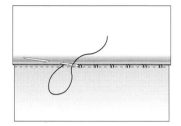

book, most of the soft sculpture projects call for slip-stitching to close the small area of a seam left unsewn so the fabric can be turned right sides out and stuffed with filling. Before you begin the stitches, gently press the fabric under so the seam allowances match. Then, begin by picking up several fabric threads just below the folded edge. Arrange the thread's knot so that it's inside the seam and will not show. Slip the needle inside the fold for about 1/4 inch directly above the stitches you just put on the needle, then bring the needle out and pick up a few more threads below the fold. Continue until you've secured all of the unsewn area.

Staystitching — Staystitching is used to prevent the fabric from stretching when you anticipate handling the fabric a lot during the pinning and sewing process. Staystitches are usually just a single row of machine stitches at your regular stitch length and tension.

Topstitching — Topstitching is usually done for decorative reasons in a matching or contrasting thread color. The stitch should be just a little longer than you use for regular seams to ensure ease and about 1/4 inch in from the edge. Extra rows of parallel top-stitches can be added for a custom look. Be sure to press the garment or item before stitching.

QUILTING TIPS

Patchwork — Although patchwork quilting can look difficult to a novice, most patterns can be easily pieced by a beginner. Before you begin, study the finished piece to see how it breaks down — both in shapes (two triangles pieced together to form a square, squares set on the diagonal to form diamonds, etc.) and in color (contrasting colors versus blends).

Patchwork can be done quickly with a rotary cutter and assembly line stitching. A rotary cutter allows you to cut through multiple layers of cloth (instead of the traditional two). To assembly line sew, first pin 20 or 30 pieces together and position them in a stack on your sewing machine. Stitch the seams as your normally would, but don't cut the threads in between seams. You will end up with a kite-like streamer of patchwork pieces, which you can clip apart in a minute or two.

With clothing, it often doesn't matter if you sew one seam 3/8 inch and another 1/4 inch — the garment may well still fit fine. With patchwork, though, identical seams is a must in order for the points to meet. Pressing all seams flat is especially important with patchwork quilting because unpressed or poorly pressed seams will cause unsightly bulk in the finished piece, or, worse, cause the blocks to pull or twist.

Appliqué — Appliqué is usually used in quilting when you have a shape or motif which would be very difficult to do with geometric patchwork piecing. In this book, you will be provided with an appliqué pattern. Just cut it out, press under a seam allowance, (clipping the corners if needed for turning ease), and hand baste the shape to a backing fabric. Topstitch the motif by machine around the edges and quilt over it as you would patchwork.

Quilting — the actual process of quilting, or adding texture though a series of simple running stitches, is not complicated at all — just time intensive. You can shadow quilt your design by outlining the patchwork or appliqued shapes with running stitches — or do an allover pattern. For most of the small quilting projects in this book, you won't need a hoop or large frame to keep the fabric taut. An increasingly popular option to hand quilting is machine quilting.

The Quilting Sandwich — The "sandwich", as it's commonly called, consists of a backing fabric (with right sides facing outward), a layer of batting in the center, and the pieced or appliqued fabric on top (right sides facing up). To prevent unpleasant creases and gathers, it's easier if you baste the layers together by hand in addition to pinning, before you begin quilting. For larger pieces, lots of basting at this stage will save you lots of pulled stitches later. For smaller pieces, a diagonal X will be enough.

Mitering —
Mitering is used at the corners of quilts as a finishing technique. Mitering can be awkward until you get the technique down pat, so you may wish to study the illustrations well and then practice with basting stitches before proceeding. First, turn the seam allowance or the hem nd facing to the inside and press. Open out the pressed edges.

Fold the corner diagonally across the point so the pressed lines meet, then press. Open the corner and trim it 1/4 inch from the crease. With right sides facing, fold the corner, matching the trimmed edges. Stitch on the diagonal crease. Trim the fold at the point and press the seam open. Turn and press well.

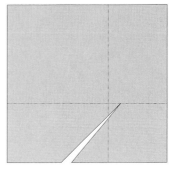

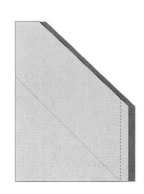

CONTRIBUTING DESIGNERS

Suzanne Koppi (pages 27, 29, and 114) teaches special education in Asheville, North Carolina. She enjoys needlework and sewing crafts, and enjoys sewing for her husband and three children.

Juanita Metcalf (pages 48, 49, 51, 54, 59, 62, 63, 70, 71, 74, 75, 90, and 91) is certified by the National Quilter's Association as a teacher and judge. She teaches workshops and gives lectures on a variety of quilting workshops. A recently retired math teacher, Juanita operates a quilt shop, Juan's Quilt Cabin, in Clyde, North Carolina, and creates specialty items on consignment.

Dot Rosenstengel (pages 19, 33, 88, 89, and 97) is an avid needleworker who lives in the mountains of North Carolina. Although cross stitch and lacemaking are her favorite pastimes, she also enjoys experimenting with other crafts.

Also thanks to . . . **Aubrey Gibson** (page 36), **Eula Haynes** (pages 106 and 107), **Carol Parks** (page 23), and **Joyce Cusick** (pages 68 and 82).

And thanks to the models . . . **Amanda Connolly** (page 90), **Marina Frazier** (page 106), **Dimitry Gaddis** (107), and **Wesley Albrecht** (page 97).

INDEX